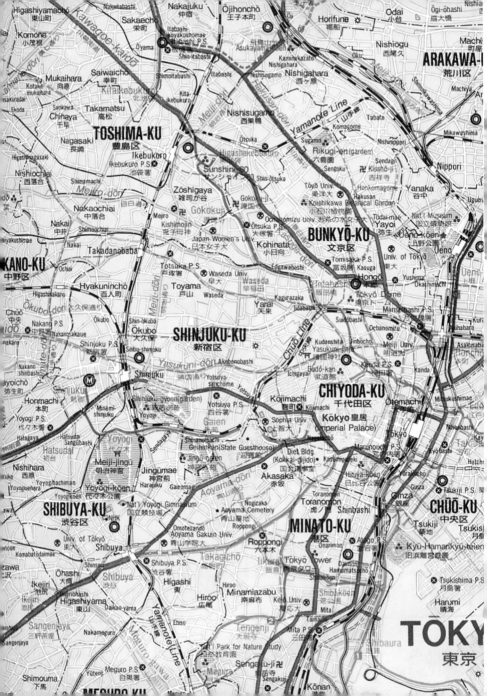

TOKYO
COCKTAILS

AN ELEGANT COLLECTION OF
OVER 100 RECIPES INSPIRED
BY THE JAPANESE CAPITAL

NICHOLAS COLDICOTT

CIDER MILL PRESS

BOOK
PUBLISHERS
KENNEBUNKPORT, MAINE

TOKYO COCKTAILS

13-Digit ISBN: 978-1-60433-886-7
10-Digit ISBN: 1-60433-886-5

This book may be ordered by mail from the publisher. Please include $5.99 for postage and handling. Please support your local bookseller first!

Books published by Cider Mill Press Book Publishers are available at special discounts for bulk purchases in the United States by corporations, institutions, and other organizations. For more information, please contact the publisher.

Cider Mill Press Book Publishers
"Where good books are ready for press"
PO Box 454
12 Spring Street
Kennebunkport, Maine 04046
Visit us online!
cidermillpress.com

Typography: GradoGradoo, Avenir, Copperplate, Sackers, Warnock

Photography Credits on page 358

Printed in China

2 3 4 5 6 7 8 9 0

CONTENTS

INTRODUCTION

It was a Brit who brought cocktails to Japan. A great-nephew of Jane Austen, no less. George T. M. Purvis was a former captain with the Royal Navy who washed up in the port of Yokohama in the 1870s, a time of great turmoil and opportunity.

In the preceding decade, Japan had mourned an emperor, overthrown a shogun, moved its capital from Kyoto to Tokyo, stripped nearly 2 million samurai of their roles and privileges, and was preparing to introduce the yen and divide into 47 prefectures. Modern Japan was taking shape.

Yokohama was attracting an international medley of merchants, entrepreneurs, tourists, itinerant criminals, and adventurers, as well as fortune-seekers from across Japan. Hotels sprang up to serve them and—though the early ones were small, rough, and frequently rowdy—the city finally got one to brag about in 1868. The International Hotel was a two-story waterfront structure that advertised the largest billiard room in town. It was the city's flagship accommodation until 1873, when the Grand Hotel appeared next door to begin a fierce rivalry.

The 45-year-old Purvis took ownership of the International the summer after the Grand appeared, and within a month had introduced something he hoped would give his hotel the upper hand: Japan's first cocktail bar. Purvis himself mixed the drinks for the first few weeks, though caricatures from the era suggest it wasn't his forte, de-

picting a sweating, disheveled man trying to throw a cocktail. An experienced pro from California arrived a month later to take over.

Purvis died just five years later, so he never had to witness the rivals next door stealing the cocktail scene. In 1889, the Grand's owners hired a new general manager with an impressive hospitality resume. Louis Eppinger had emigrated from Germany to the US as a teenager and spent decades working in or managing saloons and hotels up and down the West Coast. Once in Yokohama, Eppinger ordered a renovation of the Grand, adding fancy balconies, a 300-seat dining room, in-room air coolers, and a billiard room with a bar, saying he wanted the place to be on a par with Europe's famed Grand Dame hotels.

Eppinger also introduced his guests to two drinks that would become iconic, the Bamboo and the Million Dollar (see pages 84 and 87, respectively), and trained many of the people who would become instrumental in creating Tokyo's cocktail scene.

Around the turn of the 20th century, the social elites in the capital were hungry for international culture. They frequented milk bars, beer pubs, and even a rum hall. They smoked cigars, dined on Western fare such as croquettes and Dutch meat pies, and drank Cognac and whisky with geisha. But they had to wait until 1910 for cocktails.

That's when the French-themed café Maison Konosu (as in Connoisseur) opened in Tokyo's Nihonbashi district, offering French cuisine, café au lait, glasses of punch, and cocktails. The following year, three more cafés—Printemps, Paulista, and Lion—opened in nearby Ginza with similar blueprints.

Printemps, modeled on a Parisian café, was a salon for diarists, painters, and playwrights. Paulista was founded by a coffee importer and was closer to the modern conception of a café. Lion, inspired by Britain's J. Lyons & Co. tea shops, had the best bartender, Shogo Hamada, who had trained with Eppinger and was Japan's first homegrown bar star.

By 1930, there were 600 cafés and bars in Ginza, with Lion and upstart rival Café Tiger leading the pack. The district was bustling, but the intellectuals who had cultivated that chic were growing disgruntled.

"Country bumpkins with no connection to the town are wandering around wide-eyed with their families, pushing out the people who have made Ginza their garden," wrote novelist Rintaro Takeda in 1934. Every generation since has issued the same complaint.

The intellectuals didn't abandon Ginza; they just moved to the backstreets and frequented smaller establishments.

Then came the war, and the government banned most bars, cafés, restaurants, and anything with a hint of foreignness. A select few places were converted into *kokumin sakaba* ("national taverns"), where people lined up for their ration of one beer or a cup of sake.

Ginza Street, Looking North, Tokyo
(東京) リ通座銀頭

In the immediate post-war years, with most of the restrictions still in place, there were two very different drinking cultures. The occupying forces were enjoying cocktails and fine spirits in the bars and hotels they had taken over. Locals, on the other hand, were forced to buy booze on the black market. Few could afford the authentic liquor, sold at markups of around 1,000 percent, but they could buy gut-rot shochu or a moonshine nicknamed *bakudan* ("bomb liquor"). The latter was produced by diluting methyl alcohol that was intended to be used in jet fuel but was easy to steal from airfields after the war. Many people died from drinking it.

The restrictions were lifted in 1949, and the following year whisky distiller Kotobukiya opened a bar in Ikebukuro that would grow into a chain that served the most iconic drink of the era: the Tory's Whisky Highball, or Torihai for short (see Highball History, page 62). The other big drink of the decade was the Gin Fizz, which cost twice as much as a Torihai but was considered more sophisticated. Authors name-dropped it in novels the way Raymond Chandler wrote of Gimlets and Ian Fleming used Martinis.

From 1959 to 1964, Tokyo was in a construction frenzy to prepare for the world's first live-televised Olympics. Around 30,000 people were expected to fly in, and the city—hardly a tourist destination at the time—didn't have half that many hotel beds. While some crews built highways, subways, and stadiums, others erected the Palace Hotel, the New Otani, the Okura, the New Japan, the Tokyo Prince, and the Hilton. These new luxury hotels assembled elite bartending teams, and some became academies of cocktail talent that would shape the industry long after the athletes and spectators went home.

From 1968, Japan began liberalizing a host of trade categories under pressure from the US and the IMF. The policymakers slashed tariffs on gin first, then bourbon, brandy, wine, vermouth, liqueurs, and finally Scotch.

It was a starting pistol for a more exciting cocktail scene. Suddenly Sidecars and Manhattans were as popular as Fizzes and Highballs. And the customer base diversified. "This was when women could finally go to bars without being viewed as having loose morals," says Ikuo Hiraki, who worked in Shinjuku Mammoth, part of a chain of 1,000-seat bars that opened at 5 p.m. and did a roaring trade serving people on their way to dinner or the cabaret.

The 1980s are often portrayed in the West as the darkest decade for cocktails—the era of peach schnapps, powdered sour mix, and smutty cocktail names. In Japan, it was more noteworthy as the time fresh limes became commonplace. It was *possible* to buy them before

that, but they were rare and crushingly expensive. One Japanese cocktail book published in 1968 described them for the reader as "like a lemon but smaller and green." When the imports started flowing, so did the Daiquiris and Margaritas.

In the latter half of the decade, things got a little exuberant. Banks were exceedingly loose with their credit, the Nikkei index tripled in four years, and real estate prices went stratospheric. It was dubbed the "bubble era," and the *Harvard Business Review* said at the time: "The Japanese can now afford to buy whatever they want that is for sale in capital, financial, manufacturing, high-technology, knowledge-intensive, distribution, processing, and services industries anywhere in the world. And they can afford to outbid anyone else who might want it."

People could afford whatever they wanted to drink, too, and their tastes were ostentatious. "Liquor had to be foreign and expensive," says Kiyohachi Sato, who was working in a now-gone Ginza bar called King George. "Macallan and Royal Household whiskies were very popular. Nobody wanted to drink a cocktail made with standard spirits." Akihiro Sakoh, who began bartending in that era, remembers people drinking Royal Household like water and ordering prestige whiskies mizuwari style.

In 1991, Japan's finance ministry hiked interest rates and plunged the country into a decade of deflation. No more flashy spending, everyone was saving. And perhaps it was that atmosphere that prompted bartenders to look more seriously at the jigger. The old guard had viewed the measuring cup as something akin to training wheels or water wings. To the younger generation, though, measuring with precision was just good sense and a jigger can be handled as elegantly as any other tool. Star Bar Ginza's Hisashi Kishi says one of his motivations for entering cocktail contests, jigger in hand, was to prove that precision was important. "A pâtissier measures their ingredients," he says. "Why wouldn't we?"

The 21st century has been about schisms and cross-pollination. Tomoyuki Kitazoe was the first top bartender in Tokyo to embrace the term "mixology." He trained in Ginza in the 1990s but left the district at the end of the decade to explore a more playful style in the less buttoned-up neighborhood of Nishi Azabu, first in Bar Kasumicho Arashi, then Bar Rage, then a family of bars that stretched at one point to Singapore.

"I spent a decade learning the classics," he says. "But traditions are supposed to be handed down for each generation to adapt. For me, mixology is a way to build on the traditions."

Kitazoe revised standard recipes using fresh fruit, wild herbs, vinegars, and spices. It's a mild form of mixology by today's standards, but it proved incredibly influential, and Nishi Azabu became the nucleus of a mixology scene.

It was far from the death knell for orthodox bartending, though. In fact, the classicists were about to experience a new level of acclaim. From 2008, foreign media began reporting effusively about the style and scrupulous technique of the traditional Japanese bartender, and after a century in which cocktail ideas flowed strictly from West to East, suddenly it was a conversation.

Two names appeared in almost every story: Uyeda and Ueno.

Kazuo Uyeda is the taciturn old master who laments that gentlemen no longer wear jackets to bars. At Ginza Tender, Bar L'Osier, and a Suntory-run bartending school, he trained many of the best cocktail makers in Tokyo today.

In 2010, Uyeda flew to New York to give a talk about cocktail technique. Tickets were $675 apiece. The event sold out, and, says organizer Greg Boehm, "Almost every person in that room went on to become influential in their own right."

Hidetsugu Ueno of Bar High Five is a man so intolerant of alcohol

that he says drinking a whole cocktail would kill him, yet he is preter-
naturally gifted at making them, and his English fluency made him a
favorite of writers trying to make sense of the Japanese scene. As his
profile soared, he began offering staging to international bartenders
and touring the world with a condensed version of his usually lengthy
and unforgiving training process, making him arguably the most influential Japanese bartender ever.

The year that Uyeda opened Ginza Tender—1997—Japan received
4.2 million visitors. When Ueno opened Bar High Five 11 years later,
the figure had risen to 8.3 million. Then smartphones took off, Instagram appeared, and, more importantly for Japan's inbound numbers,
so did Chinese social media apps Weibo and WeChat. Japan's policymakers created a new tourism agency, relaxed the visa rules, put up
multilingual signage and spent heavily on conveying the message that
their country was affordable, welcoming, easy to navigate, and cool. In
2019, Japan entertained 31.8 million foreigners.

Bars that had once been hushed hideaways populated by regulars would be mentioned on a blog, a social media post or, deadliest of all, the World's 50 Best Bars list, and find themselves inundated. Bartenders added foreign favorites such as Penicillins and Sazeracs to their repertoires, got more creative with their Old Fashioneds, became more familiar with infusions, and learned how to serve a "something I've never had before."

They also learned about one-star reviews. Guests who were accustomed to walking into a bar, choosing a stool and bantering with the bartender were often nonplussed with the Japanese model that asks you to wait at the door to be acknowledged and seated, offers a listening ear rather than repartee, serves drinks at a sedate pace, and adds an entrance charge to your bill.

Those critics got their hero in 2018, when award-winning bartender Shingo Gokan rode into town and blew up the local template. "Ninety percent of Tokyo bars are too serious for me," he said. "Skillwise, technique-wise, flavor-wise it's good, but it's not really interesting. If we just keep doing it this way for the next 20 years, I think all the bars will be shutting down."

At Gokan's The SG Club, there is no cover charge, pre-batched drinks are served in a blink, and guests can stand, be loud, and mingle—all verboten in a typical Tokyo bar. The Japanese-ness is in the ingredients and the concepts. The cocktails might contain shochu, wagyu, or roasted soybean flour, and they reference local themes rather than Euro or American cocktail heritage. The monthly changing chawari tea highball, for example, is a creative reworking of the tea-and-liquor staple of izakaya menus. Twenty years from now . . . Tokyo will still be a place where bartenders sweat the details of a Martini or Manhattan, but The SG Club and sister bar The Bellwood have proven there is a thirst for modern cocktails in casual settings.

This story-so-far ends in 2020 with the arrival of the COVID-19 virus. In one swipe, it retired a generation of bartenders. Septua-, octo- and nonagenarians who fell into the most at-risk category exited the industry en masse, with the notable exception of 74-year-old Takao Mori, who instead opened a second bar, albeit without his first choice of head bartender, the 90-year-old Yuzo Fukushima, whose family ordered him to retire.

Most cities make do without such veteran bartenders as a matter of course. But Tokyo has always been a place where you can pull up a seat, order a Gin Fizz, and ask your barkeep about the postwar years or the original Olympic frenzy. Those days are gone now. The question is how deep the cut goes and how many of the capital's best bars will survive a period of masked bartenders, disinfectant sprays, and severely diminished footfall.

JAPANESE BARTENDING

Picture a street lined with bars and restaurants. At one end is a casual spot in which you can order wine by color alone. Next door, when you ask for a red, the waiter will offer you medium- or full-bodied. Further along, in a fancier place, a sommelier will ask about *cépage* and New World or Old. But if you keep walking, right at the very far end of the street is a quiet place where the

owner engages you in a conversation and pours you a glass of Romanée-Conti.

This was how Star Bar Ginza owner Hisashi Kishi explained the purpose of his bar. "Most people don't need to go far down that street to be content. Many will enjoy the wine in that first bar," he said. "But some people appreciate fine wines, and that's where I want to be. I want to make the Romanée-Conti of Gimlets."

We were discussing what defines Japanese bartending. He said the popular perception—that it's a time capsule, a snapshot of the 1920s—is wrong. That wouldn't work, he explained, because people's diets and palates are so different now, not to mention the ingredients, access to refrigeration, and so much more. So they have to keep thinking, refining, improving.

Kishi considers himself a creative bartender, but his is not the kind of creativity that you can see in a photograph. It's more like precision engineering, all under the hood, and the customer no more needs to hear about it than the Romanée-Conti drinker should understand viticulture.

Across Tokyo, bartenders are trying to fine-tune famous cocktails, speeding up or slowing down their stirs, rethinking how they move a shaker and juice a fruit, pondering whether the ice in their mixing glass should be shiny or coarse, how hard it should be, and whether they should shorten their stir in the summer. The techniques matter so much that few top bartenders mix with top-shelf spirits. Brands such as Beefeater, Bacardi, Courvoisier, and Dewars are the primary colors of a Japanese bar, and the artisanship is in the aeration, dilution, temperature control, and other kinds of chemistry.

In Bar cafca. [sic], Hirokazu Sato stirs a Manhattan so slowly that you might wish for a radar gun to check that the spoon really is moving. He is aiming to blend the ingredients and draw a little water from the ice to open up the aroma, without over-chilling the drink. In

Bar Sherlock, Takeshi Yoshimoto shoots for the same goal with precisely the opposite method (see page 329). Both make Manhattans as good as any you will ever taste.

Some bartenders say you should pour the vermouth before the rye. Others will argue the opposite. Daisuke Ito of Land Bar Artisan says the way you insert the spoon and begin the stir makes all the difference. For a digestif cocktail such as a Manhattan, insert the spoon at the near side of the mixing glass and begin with a pushing motion. For an aperitif such as a Martini you must start at the far side with a pulling motion. Even Ito concedes that it sounds improbable. "If you write about it in Japanese, people here will mock me," he says. Nevertheless, I have filmed him, timed him, scrutinized his movements, and tasted drinks side by side. A Manhattan pushed for 20 seconds arrives rich, smooth and mellow; begin with a pull and the cocktail comes with a sharp bite. With Martinis, the difference is visible: one is crystal clear, the other opaque. It may be related to the mechanics of a hand, or it might only be true of his particular stir. Either way, it is an extraordinary demonstration of how a detail can make or break a cocktail.

This fanatical focus works partly because guests enjoy the pursuit of perfection, but also because the reason for visiting a bar is quite different from the motivations that prevail in New York, London, or Singapore. In Tokyo, in a traditional bar, the guests are buying a moment of peace, refinement, and fantasy.

Kazuo Uyeda wrote in his book *Cocktail Techniques* that "cocktails represented a bottomless well of dreams and romance." Sip a Jack Rose and you're Jake Barnes at the Crillon Hotel in Hemingway's *The Sun Also Rises*, far from the grinding reality of Tokyo office work and long commutes on crowded trains. For this reason, some bartenders seek out underground locations. "They cut you off more from daily life," says Kazuma Matsuo (see page 140). "We only considered basements when we were looking for a location [for Bar Landscape]."

And so bar rooms are usually quieter in Japan than abroad, and the rules are a little more forbidding but their purpose is to protect that exquisite experience the guests are looking for.

The week after Hisashi Kishi gave me his wine bar analogy, I went to visit him and asked for "a Romanée-Conti of Gimlets." He looked at me blankly and said, "What does that mean?" Well, he might have forgotten the analogy, but he made me an outstanding Gimlet.

JAPANESE HOSPITALITY

When you leave Yanagikoji Bar Maruume (see page 192), your bartender will escort you outside and wait on the street until you are out of sight. If you turn around, they will bow and you should too.

In bars owned by Yuichi Hoshi, staff will see you to the elevator, wait for the doors to close, then hurtle down the staircase as fast as they can to ensure that they are waiting for you at ground level, to bow once more. For the bartenders of Bar Hoshi No. 9, it means outpacing an elevator down nine flights.

These are the eye-catching, unforgettable examples of Japanese hospitality, but there are many more details that the keenest eye would never notice.

Many bartenders will polish every bottle on the shelves, every day—even the ones at the back that never get touched—because, as Atsushi Yoshikawa of Bar Legacy puts it, the way you clean sets the tone for everything else you do. If you cut corners on polishing the bottles, that mindset will infect all the rest of your work.

The word for Japanese-style hospitality is *omotenashi*, meaning, roughly, "nothing hidden." It derives from the tea ceremony that has influenced Japanese service and aesthetics for five centuries.

In feudal times, an educated person was expected to know the Way of Tea, and just as cocktails today offer a moment of calm, a ceremonial bowl of tea could take a samurai's mind off life's literal battles.

Students of tea ceremony learn the correct way to open a door, enter a tearoom, draw water from a pot, wipe a bamboo ladle, and so much more. Every movement is as elegant as it is prescribed. Tea master Hōunsai, former head of one of Japan's three main schools of tea, once wrote that the formalized movements "may seem at first troublesome, but without them, the attention of the host would be diverted to such matters as what is the most efficient movement of the body, what shall I do next, how shall I make the charcoal fire, etc. In truth, the unvarying nature of the movements enhances their capacity to reveal individual character."

You can see echoes of this idea in sushi restaurants, department stores, train stations, and Japanese bars. A bartender's movements are fluid and graceful, but also instinctive and liberating.

Toshiaki Tanaka of Bar Caesarean (see page 69), whose grandmother taught tea ceremony, says you can judge a bartender by his *nagorite*, an obscure tea term that refers to the way you withdraw your hand. "If you pull away too fast after serving a drink, you're showing no respect," he says.

Omotenashi is also why bartenders place the bottles on the counter to show you what will be going into your drink. Nothing hidden.

"The process matters a lot. In tea ceremony, *ikebana*, the way you do things is very important. Abroad you find great bartenders using pre-mixed ingredients because speed is important. Their focus is on speed and quality," says Manabu Ohtake (see page 191), former Diageo World Class global champion. "In Japan, it's about process and quality."

TRAINING

In 2019, Brian Kientz celebrated three years of working at Bar High Five but was still waiting to mix his first drink. In Ginza, the land of long apprenticeships, that's not unusual, except for one thing: Kientz came to the bar with 12 years of bartending experience. In his native New Orleans, he worked at the famed Sazerac Bar and was head bartender at Tujague's, the birthplace of the Grasshopper cocktail.

But you leave your credentials at the door when you join a bar like High Five. Kientz rolls the hand towels, straightens the coasters, polishes the bottles, and vacuums the bar. When service starts, he picks up his notepad to take orders and his cloth to polish the glasses.

He says he used to feel like the young Caine in the opening scene of the '70s TV show *Kung Fu*. The boy turns up each day at the gates of the Shaolin monastery, asking to be allowed in for training. Each day he is sent away, but returns in sun or rain until the monks are convinced of his humility and desire.

"Everything here has a *kata*, a right way of doing things," he says. "Even the vacuum cleaning." But rarely is the reason for that kata made explicit. "You just have to bang your head against a wall until you get it," he says.

One day he realized that the way they were peeling the fruit was the same motion as carving an ice ball. He had been practicing without knowing. Wax on, wax off.

In Bar Caesarean, Toshiaki Tanaka says it's essential not to make the learning process too easy. "If you do that, people remember nothing." He says if an apprentice makes a drink that isn't up to par, the most he will say is "That's interesting," and leave them to figure out why. In High Five, Ueno is only slightly more forthcoming. "He'll say 'sweet' or, the one I hate, 'needs more air,'" says Kientz.

In June 2020, the persistence paid off, the monastery door cracked open a little, and Kientz was allowed to make his first cocktails for guests at Bar High Five.

TECHNIQUES

OPENING A BOTTLE
The late, influential Shogo Hamada (see page 87) wrote that you should hold a knife against the seal and rotate the bottle, because "any other way looks ugly."

REMOVING A CAP
Place the cap of a bottle against the palm of one hand. Hold the bottle with the other hand. Twist both at the same time, and palm the cap the way a magician hides a coin. Keep it in your hand until you are finished using the bottle.

MEASURING WITH A JIGGER
The Japanese jigger is tall and slim. Hold it between the index and middle fingers and tilt it away from you. Never hold between thumb and forefinger like a jar of salt.

SHAKING A COCKTAIL
Shake a cocktail to combine liquids of significantly different densities, such as a spirit with juice, cream, or egg. Unless otherwise stated, all the recipes in this book were designed for a three-piece Cobbler shaker. There are a multitude of ideas about how to move a shaker and how much ice to use, but you should be considering how much water you want, how much air you want, and how cold you want the drink to be.

Stirring a cocktail

Add ice to a mixing glass, but do not overfill. Pour water over the ice, stir briefly and strain to remove fine particles. Add the ingredients and stir with a cocktail spoon as smoothly and silently as possible. For many drinks, the aroma will tell you when it is ready to pour.

Double Straining

A cobbler shaker has a built-in strainer, but if you wish to remove finer particles or ice chips, pour through a fine-mesh strainer.

Creating a sugar or salt rim

Pour the sugar or salt into a small saucer. Take half a lemon or lime. Place the glass against the citrus at a 45° angle and rotate. Kazuo Uyeda says this ensures that you moisten the rim in the most uniform way. Place upside down in the saucer. Lift and tap to remove excess sugar or salt.

Expressing citrus

Cut a thumb-sized piece of peel from a citrus fruit. Hold it between your thumb and index or middle finger with the zest pointing away, press it together, and waft. The late Kiyoshi Imai (see page 174) said it's important to do this near the drink, not above it, because the citrus notes will spray forward but the bitter oils fall straight down. Imai said a 45° angle, several inches from the glass, was correct.

— HOW TO DRINK LIKE A TOKYOITE —

- Lose your friends. Cocktail bars in Tokyo are small. Many won't accept groups larger than four, even if the room is empty.

- That hand towel is for your hands. It's considered uncouth to wipe your face with it. But if it's summer and no one is looking . . .

- Read the room. If it's hushed, you should be too. If your neighbors are chatty, make friends.

- You probably can't have a Ramos Gin Fizz. You can have a Kaikan Fizz, though (see page 91). What's popular abroad isn't always big in Japan.

- When the bartender begins to mix your drink, sit tight. That's not the time for a toilet break.

- Europeans: don't toast with "chin chin." It's Japanese slang for the male appendage.

- Don't clink glasses. Yours might be a Baccarat piece from the 1930s and your host won't thank you for chipping it.

- Make a cross with your index fingers to ask for the check. When it arrives, hide your sticker shock.

- After drinks, ramen.

bar Dolphy

and Bar
artisan

BAR ORCHARD
GINZA

Bar
Caesarean

Sanlucar
BAR

Bar Sherloch

3F BAR
COCKTAIL WHISKY
GIN   CHAMPAGNE
VERMOUTH RUM

Cielo

2F BAL

OPEN

LE ZINC

22

THE MASTERS

MARTINI + GIMLET + CAMPARI SODA +

GIN & TONIC + SIDECAR +

WHITE LADY + HIGHBALL

"Mixology is like going to a disco. It's fine for young people, but when you get older it just gets annoying."

—HISASHI KISHI, STAR BAR GINZA

Tokyo's cocktail scene is, at its core, classic. And in this world there's an accolade greater than any trophy or appearance on a Best Bars list. The classicists want to be recognized as the master of a timeless cocktail.

Not many have managed it. When everyone in the city is refining the same core recipes, you need to be exceptional to rise to the top.

It helps to have a signature technique: a hard shake (see page 39), an infinity shake (page 50), or a hundred-time stir (page 34), for example. And it helps if you work in the Ginza district, where alcohol industry people drink, and the density of elite bars is so ridiculously high that word spreads fast. There is a little bit of jockeying, too, with bartenders talking up their signature drinks. But in the end, as White Lady maestro Hidetsugu Ueno says, "*You* can't decide. The people decide."

Not every classic has a king. The Negroni, the Old Fashioned, the Margarita, and the Bloody Mary are all up for grabs. But here is Tokyo's current Magnificent Seven.

— MARTINI —

MORI BAR, GINZA

I told Takao Mori that his famous Martini was deliciously complex. He chuckled and told me it wasn't.

Actually, it was, but to understand his point of view you need to know his history.

Early in his career, back in the 1960s and '70s, he was making Martinis with a high-proof Gordon's gin, as were most of his peers. Gradually, though, he began to feel that the quality of the gin was slipping, and he asked Japan's three big beverage companies to find him something better. In 1987, Kirin Seagram suggested Boodles and it was a bull's-eye. It had weight, depth, and the touch of sweetness that he says a Martini gin needs. It was also tough enough to survive in a freezer.

Mori likes to chill the gin to -4°F (-20°C), at which point, he says, "It's dead."

He then revives it with a dash of orange bitters, a splash of vermouth, and 100 brisk rotations with ice in a mixing glass. He stirs not to chill the drink, but to wake it up, bringing the temperature up to around 19°F (-7°C), with each rotation sending a little more water into the mix.

Japan's top bar associations all asked Mori to make Martinis for their conferences, and word quickly got around. By the time he opened his eponymous bar in 1997, he was using more Boodles than anyone else in the world, and the makers showed their gratitude by furnishing him with their formula.

Then a US firm bought Boodles and tweaked the recipe. They made it gentler, more approachable, and Mori immediately stopped using it.

He would have stopped making Martinis altogether, but his customers demanded them. He was stuck with gins he felt were too simple, too light.

Salvation of a sort came with the arrival of Japanese gins. The makers of Ki No Bi offered to create a spirit to Mori's taste. He traveled to Kyoto to help develop it, armed with his Boodles recipe, and in 2017, his 50th year as a bartender, the Ki No Bi Mori edition made its debut. Precisely what's in it, nobody will say, but Mori finally had his dream gin again.

Well, not quite.

Ki No Bi's base spirit is made from rice, not grain like Boodles, and Mori says that means it's too light to live in a freezer, and thus too light for his signature stir. So he chills it in the fridge and gives it just 50 rotations. But he says Suntory's Roku gin *is* rugged enough. It goes in the freezer and comes back to life with the full hundred stirs. So there are now two Mori Martinis. I tried them side by side. The Ki No

Bi Martini was, I thought, deliciously complex and fun. The Roku version was deep and precise. Then Mori fetched a bottle of Boodles he had been hiding all these years in his freezer and made a third version. It was a bullet of flavor, dramatic and tightly focused. So Boodles was best, but all three were exceptional.

Since only the Roku Gin is available for purchase, that's the recipe presented here.

GLASSWARE: Cocktail glass

GARNISH: Olive

- 1 drop orange bitters
- 3.5 oz. | 100 ml Suntory Roku Gin (chilled to −4°F | −20°C)
- ½ teaspoon Mancino Secco Vermouth
- 1 strip of lemon peel

1. Place three large ice cubes in the mixing glass, cover them with water, and stir. Strain the water from the mixing glass.

2. Add the drop of bitters.

3. Pour the gin into the mixing glass, add the vermouth, stir rapidly 100 times, and strain into a cocktail glass.

4. Skewer the olive on a cocktail pick and garnish the cocktail with it.

5. Express the lemon peel over the drink and discard it.

When Takao Mori was young and wondering what career to pursue, he had just one criteria: it should have nothing to do with alcohol. His father ran a *ryotei*—a high-end, invitation-only restaurant—and he witnessed too much drunken misbehavior.

Mori was a talented baseball pitcher hoping to turn pro. He took a part-time job as a waiter at the Tokyo Kaikan hospitality complex and, naturally, signed up for the house baseball team. He led them to victory in their next tournament and he caught the eye of the Kaikan's charismatic bar manager, who asked Mori to join his crew. And so, in 1968, he found himself serving alcohol after all.

Two decades later he helped to open Gaslight, a bar in the government district of Kasumigaseki. Officials from the nearby Ministry of Finance would visit after work and traders streamed in when the stock markets closed. These were the heady days of Japan's bubble era and Martinis were in high demand. Gaslight became an institution and a springboard for the careers of many top Tokyo bartenders.

In 1997, Mori left to open his eponymous bar in Ginza. In 2020, at the age of 74, he opened a second, Mori Bar Gran, nearby.

In his absence, his right-hand man of 20 years, Tadakatsu Watanabe, makes the drinks. In his 2007 book, *Martini-ism*, Mori wrote that Watanabe is the only person besides him who can make a great Martini. Watanabe puts it slightly differently: "Everyone knows mine are better."

— GIMLET —

For around 50 years, Gimlets in Japan tasted a lot like Gimlets abroad. They contained gin and lime cordial in ratios varying from 1:1 to 4:1. Sometimes they had a sugar rim.

Then along came Kazuo Uyeda. After eight years training at the Tokyo Kaikan bar—a high-society hangout and a factory of bartending talent at the time—he left to open a bar for cosmetics giant Shiseido. It was conceived as a waiting bar attached to their French restaurant L'Osier, but it grew into a destination bar in its own right, and Uyeda found that his wealthy employers were willing to buy ingredients the average bartender could only dream of, such as fresh limes. In the 1970s, a lime cost about three times the hourly wage of a bartender, but Shiseido had deep pockets. He started making Gimlets with real juice and sugar syrup, because he felt that had a better sweet-sour balance. Today, that's the standard recipe throughout Japan.

Uyeda serves his Gimlets the way they did at the Tokyo Kaikan: in a coupe with a chunk of ice in the middle to keep everything cold. But he was less enamored with his mentors' shaking technique. They would hold their elbows out at right angles and thrust the shaker away and back, almost horizontally. Uyeda didn't feel comfortable with that stance, so he searched for one that suited him.

Initially, he was trying only to mix the ingredients, make them cold, and take the sharp edge off the alcohol. "Many people can't even do that. They're absolutely terrible," he says. "But I could, and it produced tiny bubbles as a result." He says those bubbles add volume, surrounding the alcohol to cushion the blow to your tongue.

TOKYO COCKTAILS — 39

When he shakes in precise semi-quavers, he looks as though he's tapping the shaker against the bulbs of traffic lights in order—red, yellow, green—and then a powerful fourth beat that would smash the yellow bulb.

In the early 1980s, magazines and newspapers started writing about it, calling it his "3-point throw." Then one of his customers started calling it a "hard shake," because it's so powerful that some of the ice shatters and ends up in your drink.

The hard shake became the most famous Japanese bartending technique of all time, but Uyeda says most people do it for the wrong reason. "Because of that name, people think it's about thrashing a shaker to get tiny ice chips, but that's not right," he says. "It's about getting bubbles. The ice is secondary."

If you wish to try the hard shake, Uyeda recommends using a combination of hard and soft ice. He uses 70 percent ultra-pure ice from his supplier and 30 percent ice cubes he makes in his freezer.

And you'll want a spirit that's not too delicious. In his 2000 book, *Cocktail Techniques*, he wrote that "in general, the more delicious a liquor is when drunk by itself, the less suited it is to the hard shake." The logic is that the shake transforms the drink, so you need strength of character, not subtleties.

He uses Gordon's, which he says has the backbone to stand up to a hard shake.

Ginza Tender closed permanently in 2020 when the COVID-19 virus hit, but Uyeda is planning to reopen in a smaller venue.

GLASSWARE: Coupe

- 1½ oz. | 45 ml Gordon's Gin
- ½ oz. | 15 ml fresh lime juice
- 1 bar spoon simple syrup

1. Fill a shaker with a mix of hard ice and "softer," homemade ice, add the ingredients, and hard shake.

2. Strain—do not double-strain—the cocktail into the glass.

3. Take one of the hard ice cubes from the shaker and place it in the center of the glass.

Kazuo Uyeda is one of the few people of his generation who actually wanted to be a bartender. His interest was piqued when he was a junior high school student and his elder brother, deciding he wanted to start making cocktails at home, installed a bar in his bedroom. A few years later, the young Kazuo moved from his home in Hokkaido to Tokyo, where he studied at the esteemed Aoyama Gakuin University and worked for a printing company. His employer gave him a room in a dormitory and he wrote home to his mother, a furniture retailer, asking her to send shelves and cabinets. She must have assumed she was sending him fittings for his suits and schoolbooks, but he used it all to build a bar in his dorm room, and on weeknights and weekends would mix drinks for his colleagues. It didn't take him long to quit the job, drop out of college, and switch to bartending full time, though it was quite a bit longer before he would break the news to his mother.

— CAMPARI SODA —

BAR SHAKE, GINZA

I know what you're thinking: It's a bitter drink with some bubbles. Pour one on the other, next recipe please. But let me convince you it's not quite that simple.

The best Campari Sodas in Tokyo, and therefore the world (sorry, Italy), are made by Masayuki Kodato in Bar Shake. He is a soft-spoken alumnus of the legendary, long-gone Bar L'Osier, where he trained with Kazuo Uyeda (see page 39). Once upon a time he looked set to become the master of the Daiquiri. His are outstanding (45 ml Bacardi, 15 ml fresh lime juice, 1 teaspoon sugar syrup; hard shake), but people gradually began talking more about his Campari Sodas. When the media got involved and ran articles about them, it sealed his reputation.

Kodato's Campari Sodas are more vivid than others, and no matter how slowly you sip, they never turn watery or warm.

Most recipes call for a highball glass full of ice. Kodato uses a Collins glass with just one small cube. "If the glass has too much ice, you finish the drink in one gulp," he says. Less ice also means less dilution, which is why Kodato's version holds its flavor for a surprisingly long time. The trick is to keep all the ingredients chilled.

There's some heresy involved, too. Kodato adds a splash of lemon juice to brighten the flavors in a way the traditional orange slice cannot. It works in cooking, and it works here too.

For the soda, Kodato says it must have a lively effervescence to impart *nodogoshi*, a term that translates roughly as "throat-tickling refreshment." He uses the Japanese brand Wilkinson.

And, finally, there's the stir: since there's plenty of fizz and very little ice to kill the carbonation, he can be more aggressive with the bar spoon, jiggling it forcefully until the Campari rises all the way to the top.

GLASSWARE: Collins glass

- **2 oz. | 60 ml Campari, chilled**
- **½ teaspoon fresh lemon juice**
- **1 (190 ml) bottle of Wilkinson Club Soda**

1. Place a small ice cube in the glass, add the Campari and lemon juice, and top with the soda.

2. Jiggle and lift the Campari with a bar spoon until the drink is fully mixed.

– GIN & TONIC –

BAR ANTHEM, GINZA

Atsushi Asakura of Bar Anthem breaks a lot of conventions when he makes his famous Gin & Tonic. He uses eight ingredients, a cocktail shaker, and more club soda than tonic. But the most radical departure is this: he says it doesn't matter what gin you use. And he's right, as long as you follow his recipe.

When he opened Anthem in 2009, he wanted to create a signature drink and the G&T was in need of an overhaul. Tonic waters in Japan were high in corn syrup, contained artificial quinine, and drowned rather than accented the flavors in the gin.

So he bought 10 kilograms of cinchona bark from a dealer of Chinese medicines and sent it to a lab to have it refined. He received so

many boxes of powder back that a decade later he still has plenty left.

This is the starting point of his G&T, just as it should be: historically, the drink was a way for British soldiers in India to consume bitter, anti-malarial quinine. Asakura builds the drink around his quinine using juniper berries, the juice and oils of a lime, a little Q Tonic (light and elegantly bitter), a little Wilkinson Tonic (more "tonicky"), a lot of soda, and gin.

He infuses the gin with the berries and lime peel, then uses a shaker to mix in the juice and cinchona powder. That latter technique got people's attention. Bloggers began writing about the Ginza bartender making G&Ts with a cocktail shaker. The internet made him famous, he says, but you don't become king of a classic with theater alone. The drink tastes as though he took the flavor matrix for a typical version of this classic and stretched it in every direction.

GLASSWARE: Highball glass
GARNISH: Lime wedge

- 1 oz. | 30 ml Infused Gin, chilled in the freezer
- 2 bar spoons fresh lime juice
- 1 pinch cinchona powder
- 3 oz. | 90 ml club soda (use an effervescent one)
- 1 oz. | 30 ml Q Tonic Water
- ½ oz. | 15 ml Wilkinson's Tonic Water

1. Place two large ice cubes in a highball glass.

2. Add the gin, lime, and cinchona powder to a shaker.

3. Strain any water from the glass, pour the soda over the ice.

4. Add two cubes of ice to the shaker, shake gently for 10 seconds, and strain into the glass.

5. Add the tonics.

6. Use a bar spoon to press the ice cubes down and let them bob up; that's enough to mix.

7. Score a criss-cross pattern into the zest of the lime wedge and garnish.

INFUSED GIN: Place 4 dried juniper berries and the peel of 1 lime in 700 ml gin and let the mixture steep for 1 day. Strain and store the gin in the freezer.

Asakura's uncle Shinjiro was chief bartender at the Imperial Hotel (see page 338) in the post-war years, as well as a cocktail book writer and head of the national bartending association. His dry Martini was reportedly a favorite of General Douglas MacArthur.

— SIDECAR —

Japan's national public broadcaster aired a show in 2016 all about Hisashi Kishi, a bartender of rare distinction. Kishi has won two world cocktail championships, is the only bartender to receive the Emperor's medal of honor, and is acknowledged by his peers to be King of the Sidecar.

After the show was broadcast, Star Bar Ginza had a full house every night and a line of people at the door. Everyone wanted to try his celebrated Sidecar. It was, he says, "the final stab to my wound."

Kishi was never a man for the limelight. Star Bar Ginza is supposed to be a hideaway for connoisseurs, not a magnet for aspiring Instagram influencers. So when the hordes arrived, Kishi disappeared. For 18 months after the show aired, he barely set foot in his bar and ordered his staff to stop serving the cocktail that was luring everyone in.

The dust has settled now—Kishi is back, his Sidecars are too, but he says he still doesn't want to be known as the guy who makes *that* drink.

Well, this is awkward.

Kishi has to be the Sidecar guy. His rich, lush versions, with masterfully camouflaged alcohol, are the best in class, thanks mostly to his technique, as well as how he gave the traditional recipe a tweak: less lemon, more Curaçao, and Grand Marnier instead of Cointreau. He does use Cointreau, but only to rinse the shaker. It's hard to imagine the rinse making much difference in this recipe. It does, though. I checked. Without it, the drink is curiously sharper, thinner, and wouldn't make a man's reputation.

The most famous ingredients are his bubbles. "Microbubbles," he calls them. They're so tiny you wouldn't know they're there, but Kishi says they temper the sweetness, make the alcohol taste milder, and give the drink its silky texture.

You could get those bubbles by shaking the life out of the drink, but then you would get lots of ice and dilution, too. Kishi puts them in before the shake, using an electric hand mixer to froth and blend the ingredients. Then he employs what's been dubbed the "infinity shake," because of the figure-of-eight loop it makes.

Hisashi Kishi was in his early 20s and working at a pocket-sized lounge called Erika in the Ginza district when one of the customers invited him to dinner. They went to a famous sushi bar and Kishi was dazzled. "The sushi was much so better than I'd ever had before," he says. After dinner, he went to work and his boss said "This seems to be a day of education, so try this," and poured him a prestige whisky. "It was probably an old Macallan or something like that," he says. Unlike the sushi, it made no great impression. "I realized I couldn't tell what made one whisky better than another," he says, and the frustration drove him to try to master his craft. Or, as he puts it: "You go to ramen shops even if you don't like the owner. I want to make cocktails so good that people will come even if they hate me."

He says it's not necessary to copy his style. He's never taught it to any of his protégés. The point is to learn the principles. You're not shaking to mix—that's already been done; you're aiming to cool without diluting, and trying to create vibrations. The shake needs to be short and intense, but don't slam the ice into the metal. When you shake a cocktail, the liquid moves faster than the ice and hits the sides first. If you can use that liquid as a cushion and whip the ice back before it crashes and chips, you aerate without making the drink watery.

Kishi says this technique is for drinks with high sugar content and low acidity. In practice, at Star Bar, it's really only for a Sidecar.

GLASSWARE: Tulip-shaped wine glass

- **Cointreau, to rinse**
- **50 ml Courvoisier Rouge V.S.O.P Cognac, chilled in the refrigerator**
- **25 ml Grand Marnier**
- **2 bar spoons fresh lemon juice**

1. Place the Cointreau in a cocktail shaker, swirl to coat, and pour out any excess.

2. Add the remaining ingredients to the shaker and froth with an electric hand mixer.

3. Add ice until the shaker is three-quarters full and shake (see above).

4. Double-strain into the wine glass.

Note: Only metric measurements are used in this recipe to honor its precision.

– WHITE LADY –

BAR HIGH FIVE, GINZA

Hidetsugu Ueno says he knew his bar's reputation had reached a
new level when a guest asked him, at the end of an evening,
what his name was. "I thought: Something's funny here. It's a small bar
on the fourth floor. You don't just wander in."

The first incarnation of Bar High Five was tiny and shared a building with more than 30 other nightlife spots. The premises had once
housed a legendary cocktail spot called Bar Cool and people say many
bartenders avoided setting up shop at that address, even after Cool
closed in 2003, for much the same reason that nobody wants to wear
the number 23 for the Chicago Bulls. As a result, the tenants in the
21st century were mainly bunny bars, hostess lounges, and other
joints with no connection to cocktail lore. It wasn't the kind of place
you would enter at random in search of a good drink.

Ueno moved into the building in 2008. He wasn't worried by the past.
After eight years working at Star Bar Ginza, he had built a name for himself as an affable, unflappable, pompadoured technician who carved ice
into the shape of diamonds and made the best White Lady in town, and
he thought the room, with an eight-seat counter and a couple of tables,
would be just right. And it was for a while. But his reputation grew. He
found himself in demand as a judge for cocktail contests around the
world. In 2011, High Five debuted on the World's 50 Best Bars list. As international media began talking about Japan's special brand of bartending,
the bilingual Ueno was best placed to explain it. In 2015, he moved a few
blocks east to a space twice the size of the original.

These days Ueno has an arsenal of original drinks to his name, including the Jazerac (see page 344), and the Black Negroni (see page

139). But, for many, his signature drink will always be the White Lady.

Start by peeling the lemon almost to the pulp. The zest contains oils that will make the juice too bitter, so get rid of it. Then slice the fruit lengthwise, carve out the bitter pith, and begin caressing the juice—gently—from each of the vesicles. The juice will be sweeter than if you had simply crushed each half.

Now pick a shaker. Ueno says a three-piece shaker with a convex bottom works best for white spirits with liqueurs. Add gin, Cointreau, and a modest ration of juice. "You can always add acidity, but you can't take it out," he says. And because your juice carries less bite than usual, you might need more of it than the traditional ratio of equal parts juice and Cointreau.

Taste, adjust, repeat until happy.

Add ice cubes until the shaker is two-thirds full and shake, hard. Then rattle vigorously as you pour. "You need ice chips inside the drink that will melt in the mouth," says Ueno. "If you just tilt and pour, the ice will just sit on the top."

The cocktail should be between 14 and 17°F (-10 and -8°C).

GLASSWARE: Cocktail glass

- 1½ oz. | 45 ml gin
- ½ oz. | 15 ml Cointreau
- ½ to ⅔ oz. | 15 to 20 ml fresh lemon juice

1. Juice a lemon using the technique described above.

2. Add the gin, Cointreau, and ½ oz. of lemon juice to a shaker; taste, and add more lemon juice if desired.

3. Add ice, shake vigorously, and strain, rattling the shaker hard, into a cocktail glass.

Like most of the best Japanese bartenders, Hidetsugu Ueno didn't want to be one. "Long hours, lousy pay, one of the lowest jobs in society," he says. And then there's the alcohol issue: he's not very good at drinking it.

His dream was to open a coffee shop. He knew how to brew Japanese style, using siphons and flannel drips, but he worried that his customers would sit for hours, reading a book, nursing their drink, eroding his profit margin, and he decided he would need to offer cocktails to earn a good living. He signed up for bartending school, and when he graduated he was 24, married, and broke, so he took the first job he was offered.

He found himself in Lounge Bar Nobuko, standing in the corner cutting fruit while the women behind the bar flirted with the male regulars and poured them Highballs or *mizuwari* (whisky cut with water).

One day the owner told a guest about Ueno's cocktail skills, and the guest asked for a Martini. "But we didn't have any mixing glasses, cocktail glasses, or olives," he says. So he improvised, and his first professional cocktail was a gin and vermouth, stirred in an old-fashioned glass and served on the rocks. That's not how he makes them now.

— HIGHBALL —

ROCK FISH, GINZA

There wasn't much cocktail culture in the seaside town of Johencho, on the island of Shikoku, when Kazunari Maguchi was growing up there. "The only kind of bar I knew was a 'snack,'" he says, referring to kitschy karaoke lounges in which dressed-up women pour you shochu or Chivas Regal and drink at your expense.

"I wanted to open a 'snack', until I saw the movie *Cocktail*," he says. "Then I thought if I did something like that instead, I'd be more popular."

That's not exactly how it worked out, though. Maguchi's fame came from figuring out how to mix whisky with soda better than anyone else.

His story really begins with a move to Osaka and a job at a bar called Samboa. It was part of a family of bars, the first of which opened in Kobe in 1918, and all of which served an excellent whisky-soda highball. Samboa bars kept the whisky in a freezer, so the drink required no ice, which meant no dilution. Maguchi stayed there for a decade, then left to open the original Rock Fish across town. It was an instant success, but ambition still nagged at him. "I wanted to try running a bar in Ginza at least once in my life," he says. So, in 2002, he signed a contract for a space he'd never even set eyes on, and boarded a train to the capital.

For the first six months, it looked like a losing bet. "I only had one or two customers a day back then, and I was very nervous," he says. By the end of year one, though, word had spread and the bar was getting busy.

Maguchi had figured out how to improve on the Samboa highball: make the whisky bolder and the glass colder. He uses an 86-proof blended Suntory whisky, rather than the 80-proof version favored by Samboa bars, and he puts it in the freezer along with his glasses. He uses the powerful Wilkinson Club Soda, which has effervescence to spare. He lets it cascade onto the whisky, the force of gravity does the mixing, and there's no need to stir. The result is a refreshing highball that holds its flavor profile for an impossibly long time.

Suntory has twice discontinued Maguchi's favorite whisky. The first time it happened, he phoned liquor stores all over Japan to buy their remaining stock. When they did it again in 2016, he had no such worries. Maguchi doesn't know the details, and Suntory won't say, but Japan's biggest drinks company seems to be keeping the high-proof version alive exclusively for the man who makes highballs better than anyone else and won't consider using any other whisky.

Maguchi says 999 out of every thousand orders he receives are for highballs, and when his regular customers turn up he doesn't even ask what they want. And no, he never gets tired of making them.

GLASSWARE: Highball glass, stored in freezer

- 2 oz. | 60 ml Suntory Whisky (86 proof), stored in the freezer
- 1 (190 ml) bottle of Wilkinson Club Soda
- 1 strip of lemon peel

1. Pour the whisky into the glass and add the soda, pouring while holding the bottle almost vertically.

2. Express the strip of lemon peel over the cocktail and discard it.

OIL SARDINES

Kazunari Maguchi is most famous as the maestro of the Highball, but he's also the author of nine best-selling cookbooks, all of which are focused on unpretentious bar fare. His 2010 book on cooking with canned food included this signature dish.

1 can of sardines in oil
1 tablespoon sake
1 tablespoon soy sauce

Pinch of black pepper
2 teaspoons sansho peppercorns

1. Open the can of sardines and drain the oil.

2. Add the sake and soy sauce to the can.

3. Top with the black pepper and sansho peppercorns.

4. Place the can directly on a burner, cook over the lowest heat for 4 to 5 minutes, and serve.

HIGHBALL HISTORY

People have been drinking whisky highballs in Japan since at least 1905, when the book *Youshu Chougou-hou*, "The Art of Mixing Western Liquor," described the recipe as follows: "In a mid-sized fizz glass, place two or three ice cubes, add a wine glass of Scotch whisky, top with cold Vichy water. If the customer wants a different spirit, give it to them."

Back then, only the most affluent could afford Scotch, and even they might have been drinking counterfeit hooch more often than the real stuff. Fizzy water would have helped it go down.

As of 1923, Japan was making its own whisky, but it was primarily reserved for the wealthy and the military until after World War II. As the country was making the transition from austerity to economic force, the middle class could finally afford a good drink, and they wanted Western-style spirits. A company called Kotobukiya, which would later change its name to Suntory, opened a chain of bars in the 1950s to promote its cheap and cheerful Torys Blended Whisky. There were eventually more than 2,000 branches nationwide and they hosted a white-collar crowd winding down after work. In the winter, the drink of choice was Torys cut with hot water; in the summer, with soda.

In the 1970s, water was in fashion again. People wanted their whisky *mizuwari*, diluted with cold water instead of soda, and the spirit of choice was Suntory Old, a more upmarket blend than Torys.

Japan's whisky consumption peaked in 1983. Ironically, that was just as Suntory and rival distiller Nikka released their first single malts, but the world wasn't quite ready. The market went on a 26-year decline. Everyone was drinking shochu, beer, or wine. Whisky was for old men. The slump lasted until 2008, when Suntory launched a marketing campaign to convince young drinkers to order a highball, not a beer, as their opening drink.

It was a success beyond their wildest expectations. Within two years there were bars serving ready-made Suntory highballs on tap. Suntory's rivals were hawking highballs of their own, and convenience stores offered canned highballs galore. Suntory's whisky sales jumped 10 percent in one year and have been growing steadily ever since.

JAPANESE ICE

Each morning at 6:00 a.m., the vans of the Chuo Reito ice company set off around the Ginza and Nihonbashi districts, delivering the ice that Hidetsugu Ueno will carve into diamonds, Yuichi Hoshi will place in his Zacapa Martinis, and the Imperial Hotel staff will use to shake their Mount Fujis. When the elite bartenders of these districts talk about the importance of ice, most of them are talking about the same ice—the rock-hard, slow-melting, ultra-pure blocks that begin life as tap water in a factory in northeastern Tokyo.

The process begins with carbon filtering, ion exchange, and reverse osmosis to remove 99 percent of the impurities. The water then goes into 3-foot-high steel or iron canisters, which are immersed in a pool of water and calcium chloride at a temperature of 14°F (-10°C). That temperature is critical. Set it lower and the ice will form faster, but it won't be as pure. When H_2O turns solid, it creates hexagonal crystals and tries to expel the impurities that sit in the gaps between molecules. The slower you freeze, the stronger and purer the structure will be.

Inside the canisters, the ice forms at 0.1 inches per hour, driving impurities into the middle. Every 24 hours, workers pump out the water in the middle and replace it with a freshly filtered version.

The biggest threats to the clarity of ice are gaseous substances dissolved in the water. The factory gets rid of them by blasting in air—the same principle that turns cola flat if you blow into it with a straw.

After 72 hours, they winch up the canisters, tilt them, and out slides an almost 300-pound pillar of near-perfect ice. The pillars are transported each morning to Chuo Reito's facility near Ginza, where staff get to work with circular saws, carving them into smaller blocks or custom-sized cubes to fit a bar's glassware.

Some of Chuo Reito's ice ends up in the hands of world-champion bartender Manabu Ohtake at the Palace Hotel Tokyo, who says Japa-

nese bartending wouldn't be possible without cubes of this quality. "When I go abroad I can't see good ice. If you do a hard shake in another country, the ice ends up all broken and the cocktail tastes totally different."

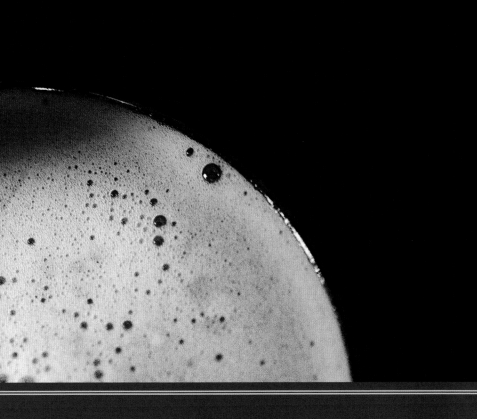

MADE IN JAPAN

YUKIGUNI + AOI SANGOSHO +

CHERRY BLOSSOM +

POLAR SHORT CUT + MY TOKYO +

BAMBOO + MILLION DOLLAR +

JACK TAR + KAIKAN FIZZ

This chapter was earmarked for all the famous cocktails created in Japan's capital. Sadly, there are none. A century of Tokyo bartending has produced an abundance of tweaks and techniques, but not one drink that has taken the world by storm. Cast the net wider, though, to cover Yokohama, Yamagata, Osaka, Nagoya, and, er, Copenhagen, and there are several drinks that have at least become part of the Japanese bartending lexicon.

To help with the list, I engaged a man who has a library of vintage recipe books and a detailed knowledge of Japanese cocktail history. Toshiaki Tanaka has been running Bar Caesarean in the bougie-boho district of Yoyogi Uehara since 1993 and is a bartender's bartender, often cited by his peers as one of the city's greats.

Tanaka trained under hard-shake inventor Kazuo Uyeda at the famed L'Osier bar, but he is far from a typical protégé. "The others all learned my style, but he always did his own thing," says Uyeda.

In fact Tanaka did learn his mentor's style, but decided that some of it wasn't for him, including that famous shake and the idea of working with spirits from the freezer.

"Mixing with freezer spirits makes it a lot easier. It's a very forgiving method. But adding ice to ice-cold liquid gives you a narrow spectrum to play with. I found that using room-temperature spirits and cooling them down worked better for me. It produces a smoother drink."

The problem is, he says, it also produces a thin drink if you aren't skillful. The trick is to use a smaller than usual shaker and ice without a wet surface, add an extra two-thirds of an ounce of liquid, and make it more spirit-forward. "The cocktails we made in Ginza suited that area," he says. "But in Yoyogi Uehara people drink in a different way. I can serve larger, stronger cocktails and strangle my guests with cotton." He means slowly get them tipsy.

Tanaka tells me he has never owned a computer or a mobile phone, but he does have one piece of modern technology: a spectrometer that he uses before service to measure the acidity in his lemons and limes in order that he can mentally adjust the balance of his pours. His guests know none of this, of course. All they see is a smiling man in a white coat who delivers drinks with exceptional texture and balance.

Since many of the recipes in this chapter were invented decades ago, and tastes change, I have included the original formulas and, where applicable, Tanaka's suggested revisions for the modern drinker.

— YUKIGUNI —

In 1959, Keiichi Iyama entered a cocktail contest run by Kotobukiya, the early incarnation of beverage giant Suntory. He was an underdog, to put it mildly. Iyama was running a coffee shop with a cocktail menu in the city of Sakata in the far north of Japan. He was competing against more than 20,000 other contestants, many with considerably more dazzling resumes. And it didn't help that he couldn't drink alcohol.

In those days, bartenders in the big cities could acquire fancy imported liquor, but coffee shop owners in Sakata had no chance. He made do with what he had, using Kotobukiya's vodka and white Curaçao, as well as a bright green lime cordial because Japan didn't import real limes back then. Iyama garnished his cocktail with a green cocktail cherry and named it *Yukiguni*—snow country—after a phrase in a poem someone had scrawled on a blackboard in his shop.

He made it through the heats and earned a trip to the finals in Tokyo. At the Sankei Hall in Yurakucho he noticed a photographer shooting his cocktail with the cherry at the bottom of the glass, not on the rim as he had specified. When he raised the issue, he was told it was deliberate: the chairman of his regional bartending association had decreed it would look better that way.

The Yukiguni won, and six decades later it's a bona fide classic in Japan, always with the cherry at the bottom of the glass. Most bartenders switch the lime cordial out for fresh lime juice, as does Tanaka, who says the combination of cordial, Curaçao, and a sugar rim is too sweet for today's drinkers.

Iyama, unsurprisingly, prefers it the authentic way. At the time of writing he is still making his Yukiguni with cordial in his coffee shop in Sakata, and at 94 is the oldest active bartender in Japan.

ORIGINAL VERSION

GLASSWARE: Cocktail glass

- Sugar, for the rim
- 1 green cocktail cherry
- 1⅓ oz. | 40 ml vodka
- ⅔ oz. | 20 ml Curaçao
- 2 teaspoons lime cordial

1. Rim a cocktail glass with sugar and place the cherry in the bottom of the glass.

2. Combine the remaining ingredients with ice in a cocktail shaker, shake vigorously, and strain into the cocktail glass.

TANAKA VERSION

GLASSWARE: Cocktail glass

- Sugar, for the rim
- 1 green cocktail cherry
- 1⅓ oz. | 40 ml vodka
- ⅔ oz. | 20 ml Cointreau
- ⅔ oz. | 20 ml fresh lime juice

1. Rim a cocktail glass with sugar and place the cherry in the bottom of the glass.

2. Combine the remaining ingredients with ice in a cocktail shaker, shake vigorously, and strain into the cocktail glass.

— AOI SANGOSHO —
(BLUE CORAL REEF)

It was 1950, and the occupying US forces had just lifted a nationwide ban on drinking. That May, the Nippon Bartenders Association held a cocktail contest and Nagoya-based bartender Hikoji Kano of Bar Eau de Vie triumphed with a cocktail inspired by the 1948 movie *The Blue Lagoon*. The reason he reached for green mint to portray a blue reef is that the words for green and blue in Japanese don't map perfectly onto English. Skies and apples are both *aoi* in Japanese, the same shade of blue as this bright green cocktail.

The original recipe called for two parts gin to one part mint liqueur, but Tanaka recommends boosting the gin for contemporary palates.

GLASSWARE: Cocktail glass
GARNISH: Maraschino cherry

- **Fresh lemon juice, for the rim**
- **1½ oz.| 45 ml gin**
- **½ oz. | 15 ml green mint liqueur**

1. Rim a cocktail glass with the lemon juice.

2. Combine the gin and liqueur with ice in a cocktail shaker, shake vigorously, and strain into the cocktail glass. Garnish with the maraschino cherry.

– CHERRY BLOSSOM –

The late Tasaburo Tao occupies a strange place in Japanese cocktail history. He is famous for creating the Cherry Blossom, a sweet, frothy drink with a brandy base that appears on menus nationwide, as well as in *The Savoy Cocktail Book*. The problem, though, is that while he did invent a drink called the Cherry Blossom, he didn't invent *that* one.

Tao had been stationed in Argentina, working for a small trading company. In the early 1920s he was on the long voyage home aboard a vessel with a cocktail bar. By the time the ship docked at Yokohama, he had decided to quit his job and open a bar of his own. He recruited bartenders from the ship and opened Café de Paris in Yokohama in 1923, just two months after a magnitude 7.9 earthquake had turned much of the city to rubble.

Later that decade, Tao entered and won a Canadian Club cocktail contest with a drink he called the Cherry Blossom. Then, in 1930, Savoy Hotel bartender Harry Craddock released the landmark *Savoy Cocktail Book* featuring a drink with the same name but a very different recipe.

The usual story in Japan is that Craddock published Tao's recipe, presumably learned from some seafaring barfly. It's an odd theory. Even the tipsiest messenger would surely remember that the Canadian Club contest-winning cocktail contained Canadian Club. Or at least whisky.

The truth is, there was a profusion of Cherry Blossoms in the 1920s and '30s, mostly containing gin or brandy. As Craddock's book became famous, his version prevailed. In Japan, bartenders conflated the world-famous recipe with the local legend.

The Yokohama bar is now known as simply Paris and is run by Tao's daughter-in-law. She has the original handwritten recipe for the Cherry Blossom, but will show it only to trusted regulars. The formula is a family secret, she says.

Not a well-kept secret though. In Bar Caesarean, Toshiaki Tanaka tells me the recipe, which he learned many years ago from Tao's wife Sachiko. And I found the same recipe in a 1931 cocktail book called *Cocktails and Fancy Drinks* (second edition), issued by a Yokohama-based publisher. It was listed as "Cherry Blossom Cocktail (Mr. Tao's formula)." The true Japanese Cherry Blossom is a lighter, fruitier sibling of the Manhattan.

ORIGINAL VERSION

GLASSWARE: Cocktail glass

GARNISH: Maraschino cherry

- ⅔ oz. | 20 ml Canadian Club Whisky
- ⅔ oz. | 20 ml cherry brandy
- ⅔ oz. | 20 ml sweet vermouth
- 1 dash maraschino liqueur

1. Combine all of the ingredients with ice in a mixing glass, stir, and strain into a cocktail glass.

2. Garnish with the maraschino cherry.

TANAKA VERSION

GLASSWARE: Cocktail glass

GARNISH: Maraschino cherry

- 1 oz. | 30 ml Canadian Club
- ½ oz. | 15 ml cherry brandy
- ½ oz. | 15 ml sweet vermouth
- 1 bar spoon maraschino liqueur

1. Combine all of the ingredients with ice in a mixing glass, stir, and strain into a cocktail glass.

2. Garnish with the maraschino cherry.

THE SAVOY CHERRY BLOSSOM

GLASSWARE: Cocktail glass

- 1 oz. | 30 ml brandy
- 1 oz. | 30 ml cherry brandy
- 2 dashes orange Curaçao
- 2 dashes fresh lemon juice
- 2 dashes grenadine

1. Combine all of the ingredients with ice in a cocktail shaker, shake vigorously, and strain into a cocktail glass.

— POLAR SHORT CUT —

By the 1950s, airplanes were sophisticated enough to travel long distances without refueling. For Scandinavian Airlines this meant they could fly from Copenhagen to Tokyo via the North Pole and shave 20 hours off the journey. They launched the new route in 1957 and held a cocktail contest to celebrate. Copenhagen-based bartender Leopold Douchar took first prize with this rich after-dinner drink. So, technically, it's a Danish cocktail, but it has been adopted as a standard by bartenders in Japan and largely forgotten everywhere else. The original recipe called for equal parts of all four ingredients. Tanaka recommends increasing the rum at the expense of the cherry brandy and Cointreau.

ORIGINAL VERSION

GLASSWARE: Cocktail glass

- ⅔ oz. | 20 ml dark rum
- ⅔ oz. | 20 ml Cointreau
- ⅔ oz. | 20 ml cherry brandy
- ⅔ oz. | 20 ml dry vermouth

1. Combine all of the ingredients in a mixing glass filled with ice, stir, and strain into a cocktail glass.

TANAKA VERSION

GLASSWARE: Cocktail glass

- 1⅓ oz. | 40 ml dark rum
- 2 bar spoons Cointreau
- 2 bar spoons cherry brandy
- ⅔ oz. | 20 ml dry vermouth

1. Combine all of the ingredients with ice in a mixing glass, stir until chilled, and strain into a cocktail glass.

– MY TOKYO –

Tokyo first hosted the Olympics in 1964 and Suntory held a cocktail contest to mark the occasion. The winning drink was the work of Osaka-based bartender Yoshiaki Ueda. Seen from above, it resembles the national flag of Japan. The drink is still famous in Osaka but rarely sighted in Tokyo now.

GLASSWARE: Cocktail glass

- Sugar, for the rim
- 1 maraschino cherry
- 1 oz. | 30 ml whisky
- ⅔ oz. | 20 ml Grand Marnier
- 2 bar spoons fresh lime juice

1. Rim a cocktail glass with the sugar.

2. Place the cherry in the glass.

3. Combine the remaining ingredients with ice in a cocktail shaker, shake vigorously, and strain into the glass.

— BAMBOO —

German bartender Louis Eppinger arrived in Yokohama in 1889 after a lengthy career in the United States. He had been hired to manage the Grand Hotel, one of Japan's first Western-style hotels, and train the staff to entertain visiting dignitaries with cocktails. The conventional story is that he invented the Bamboo cocktail a year or two later and it became a worldwide smash: the only truly famous drink born on Japanese soil.

It's a great story, but cocktail expert Simon Difford and the Italian blog EverythingInTheBar poked a giant hole in it. They both published articles pointing to a September 11, 1886 edition of the *Western Kansas World* newspaper that had been archived by the US Library of Congress. In a column called "Items of Interest," alongside reports of 13 milk dealers fined for selling watered-down milk, and news of a cigar maker offering to go over Niagara Falls in a beer keg for $500, is the story that "a new and insiduous (sic) drink has been introduced by some Englishman, and is becoming popular in New York bar-rooms. It consists of three parts sherry to one part vermouth, and is called 'bamboo.'" So Mr. Eppinger certainly knew the drink when he sailed to Yokohama three years later. I won't strip him of authorship yet, though. Many Japanese accounts of Eppinger describe him as an Englishman, and it seems plausible that 19th-century Kansans made the same mistake.

Every bartender in Tokyo has an opinion on the right kind of sherry for a Bamboo. Tanaka goes with Manzanilla, which he says gives a more precise flavor. At the Hotel New Grand, the successor to Eppinger's old workplace, they use Fino.

GLASSWARE: Cocktail glass

- 1⅓ oz. | 40 ml sherry
- ⅔ oz. | 20 ml dry vermouth
- 1 dash orange bitters

1. Combine all of the ingredients with ice in a mixing glass, stir, and strain into a cocktail glass.

— MILLION DOLLAR —

The Million Dollar was *the* cocktail of 1920s Japan. So much so that when playwright Kan Kikuchi founded the monthly magazine *Bungei Shunju* in 1923, he came up with the slogan "If it's alcohol, it's a cocktail; if it's a cocktail, it's a Million Dollar; and if it's a magazine, it's *Bungei Shunju.*" On the Imperial Hotel's bar menu in 1930 it was one of just 10 cocktails listed, and was twice the price of a Martini or Manhattan.

The drink became famous in the Ginza district at the Café Lion. The "café" in the name is misleading: the Lion was all about eating and boozing, and it drew a gregarious crowd of artists and socialites who were dazzled by the sweet and tangy cocktail and the opulence of using egg white in a drink. The man who served them was Shogo Hamada, nicknamed Mr. Bartender, who had learned the ropes, and that recipe, at the Grand Hotel in Yokohama. Hamada told people the Million Dollar was invented by his former boss, Louis Eppinger, who came up with the recipe after dreaming about a stash of $1 million. There is a conflicting origin story that claims the cocktail was invented at the Raffles Hotel in Singapore, but if you're drinking in Tokyo, you'd be wise not to mention it.

Early recipes called for Plymouth Gin, but most bartenders now use a London Dry. Tanaka goes with Gordon's and says the trick is to use a room temperature egg and whip it before shaking.

- 1 egg white
- 1 oz. | 30 ml gin
- ½ oz. | 15 ml sweet vermouth
- 2 bar spoons pineapple juice
- 1 bar spoon grenadine

1. Whip the egg white in a cocktail shaker.

2. Add ice and the remaining ingredients to the shaker, shake vigorously, and strain into a cocktail glass. Garnish with the pineapple slice.

— JACK TAR —

BAR WINDJAMMER

The most unlikely creator of a Japanese classic is former US naval officer Jimmy Stockwell, who landed in Yokohama in 1972 after a stint in Vietnam. He opened Bar Windjammer and created a drink based on his naval heritage that has become part of Japanese drinking lore, as well as a byword for hard drinking. Bar Windjammer is still open and now run by Jimmy's son Jeff. It's large, informal, and friendly, with nautical themes galore and an excellent in-house jazz band.

GLASSWARE: Old Fashioned glass

GARNISH: Lime wedge

- 1 oz. | 30 ml 151-proof rum
- ¾ oz. | 25 ml Southern Comfort
- ¾ oz. | 25 ml fresh lime juice

1. Combine all of the ingredients with ice in a cocktail shaker, shake vigorously, and strain into an Old Fashioned glass filled with crushed ice. Garnish with the lime wedge.

VARIATION: For a long version of the Jack Tar, use a highball glass and ginger ale as the mixer.

— KAIKAN FIZZ —

The Imperial Hotel was the first place in Tokyo to serve a gin fizz with milk, but the nearby Tokyo Kaikan made it legendary. The Kaikan opened in 1922 as a multi-purpose entertainment complex with banquet halls, conference rooms, restaurants, and a bar. In 1945, the occupying Allied Forces set up their headquarters a block away, commandeered the Kaikan, and turned it into The American Club of Tokyo.

The venue hosted military officers from morning to night and their appetites for drinking soon overwhelmed the bartenders. Extra staff were rushed in from the nearby Imperial Hotel, which was under the same management, and they introduced a white gin fizz they had been serving at the Imperial Bar. The drink proved a phenomenon at the Kaikan. On the palate, it's a deliciously creamy version of the standard gin fizz. To the eye, it's a glass of milk, giving the officers cover to imbibe at whatever hour they pleased.

The drink became more associated with the Kaikan than the Imperial Bar, and these days most bartenders call it the Kaikan Fizz or the Morning Fizz. Some call it the MacArthur Fizz, because General MacArthur reportedly enjoyed it. And when Kaikan bartender Kiyoshi Imai (see page 174) moved to the Palace Hotel, he took the recipe with him and named it the Special Gin Fizz. It remains at the top of their menu today.

The Tokyo Kaikan's Main Bar still serves the namesake drink from 11:30 a.m. There was, however, an even better place to drink one, until spring 2020. It was called Y&M Kisling and it was conceived as a collaboration between Takao Mori of Mori Bar (see page 34) and

Mitsugi Yoshida, who had worked alongside Imai and succeeded him as head bartender at the Palace Hotel's Royal Bar.

Mori soon found himself under pressure to spend more time at his namesake bar nearby, so he asked old friend Nobuo Abe to step in. And when Yoshida passed away in 2014, Abe became the city's greatest proponent of the Kaikan Fizz.

Abe was originally an accountant. His career took a bizarre turn when his employer, who also owned a cabaret venue, told him the nightspot was understaffed and he had to pitch in. Abe found himself enthralled by the bar culture he saw there—and the dapper head barman—and decided to switch careers. Like most people of his generation, he began on what was called the "soft" side of the industry, learning to brew coffee, whip cream, and make chocolate parfaits, before transitioning to what was called the "dry" side, where the alcohol was.

Abe went on to become chief bartender at the palatial New Otani Hotel, earned a Guinness World Record for largest Champagne tower (3,795 glasses, for a television show challenge), and retired in 2005 at the age of 66. "I was looking forward to doing nothing, and just living off my pension," he says. Then Mori called, so he donned the cream blazer again.

In some bars, if you let a Kaikan Fizz sit, it will split, as the lemon juice and milk eventually come to blows. When Abe makes them, that never seems to happen. Abe says you have to shake with ice until the liquid reaches 23°F (-5°C). After half a century of making drinks, he says he can tell exactly when that happens. His middle finger, wrapped around the shaker, is his thermometer.

Then it's a matter of how vigorously you jiggle the bar spoon as you pour the soda. If you're too timid, the milk will split. Go too hard and the drink will be flat.

Abe's recipe isn't as precise as some. He varies the gin content according to the customer, their demeanor, and whether he thinks they like their drinks strong.

Or he did until the spring of 2020, when he finally got his retirement at the age of 81.

GLASSWARE: Highball glass

- 1⅓ to 1⅔ oz. | 40 to 50 ml Gordon's London Dry Gin, depending on the guest
- ½ oz. | 15 ml fresh lemon juice
- 1 bar spoon simple syrup
- 1 oz. | 30 ml milk
- Club soda, to top

1. Combine the gin, juice, syrup, and milk with ice in a cocktail shaker, shake vigorously, and strain into a highball glass filled with ice.

2. Top with soda, rattling the drink vigorously with a bar spoon as you pour.

DAYTIME DRINKING

STRAWBERRY COCKTAIL +

IRISH COFFEE +

REVERSED MANHATTAN +

BELLINI 95 + HAVANA MARTINI +

GIMLET HIGHBALL +

MYOUGA GIN & TONIC + DOT LINE +

YOKOTA + SHERLOCK

When Kiyoshi Shimbashi opens Sanlucar Bar at 2:00 p.m., he often finds a line of people waiting outside. "We probably do better in the afternoon than the evening," he says, and explains that he opens that early because he couldn't think of any reason *not* to, and he appreciates the decorum of daytime drinkers.

At the same hour, Daisuke Ito opens Land Bar Artisan in Shimbashi. In the afternoon he welcomes journalists from nearby newspaper offices, salarymen sneaking a Martini on their way to or from a meeting, and "moms waiting to pick up their kids from kindergarten."

Meanwhile, in Shibuya, Hiromichi Itabashi opens Bar Rocaille at that hour to take advantage of the sunlight that streams into his room, and because there are always people looking for a drink in his cosmopolitan district.

In Yotsuya, Yusuke Takamiya established all-day gelato store, coffee shop, and cocktail bar Tigrato because he wanted to bring more diversity to bar culture: "I realized that talented women were quitting the industry when they had children, so I thought I could make a space where they could work the hours that suited them." He begins serving cocktails at 2:30 p.m.

Meanwhile, Kazunari Maguchi knows that people will drink his highballs at any time of day, so he has gradually moved his hours forward. Rock Fish (see page 59) opens at 3:00 p.m. on weekdays, 2:00 p.m. on weekends, and closes early, because those are the hours that work for him.

If you're in Tokyo, the sun is shining, and you want a drink, here is your guide.

— STRAWBERRY COCKTAIL —

AGRO@FORESTRY, YUTENJI

Mixology pioneer Tomoyuki Kitazoe opened this cafe-bakery-bar in late 2020. His longtime lieutenant Satoshi Iwai runs the place and based this cocktail on a red cabbage and strawberry salad he once ate. Everything from the juice to the choice of gin is designed to make the strawberry flavor pop. He serves it, starting at 7:00 a.m., in bulbous candleholders, but a cordial glass works as well.

GLASSWARE: Cordial glass
GARNISH: Dried cabbage, gorgonzola cheese, and honey

- 1 oz. | 30 ml Koval Gin
- 3 strawberries
- 2 bar spoons fresh lime juice
- 2 bar spoons cabbage juice
- 3 drops Cinnamon-Infused White Wine Vinegar
- 3 drops extra virgin olive oil
- 1 pinch salt

1. Blend all of the ingredients with a hand mixer.

2. Pour the mixture into a cocktail shaker with ice, shake vigorously, and strain into a glass (or candleholder). Garnish with the dried cabbage, gorgonzola cheese, and honey.

CINNAMON-INFUSED WHITE WINE VINEGAR: Infuse 1 stick of cinnamon per 100 ml of vinegar for a week. Strain before using or storing.

— IRISH COFFEE —

ARRIVIAMO BAR, STARBUCKS RESERVE ROASTERY, NAKA MEGURO

In the early hours, most of the customers at the world's largest Starbucks order coffee and pastries, but up on the third floor, in Arriviamo Bar, you can often spot a local or two starting the day in style. The best seller at that hour is two-time coffee cocktail champion Shuichi Ofuchi's Irish Coffee, which has a toffee note from the dash of PX sherry.

GLASSWARE: Irish Coffee glass

- ¾ oz. | 25 ml Bushmills Black Bush Irish Whiskey
- ½ teaspoon El Candado Pedro Ximénez Sherry
- ½ oz. | 15 ml simple syrup (made with demerara sugar)
- 2 oz. | 60 ml medium-roast espresso
- Hot water, to top
- Lightly whipped cream, to taste

1. Fill the glass with hot water. When the glass is warm, discard the water.

2. Add the whiskey, sherry, and syrup and stir.

3. Add the coffee and hot water—reserving room for the cream—and stir again.

4. Float the cream on top by pouring it over the back of a spoon.

– REVERSED MANHATTAN –

FUGLEN TOKYO, TOMIGAYA

The original Fuglen Café opened in Oslo in 1963. The second branch opened 49 years later and 5,200 miles away in Tomigaya, Tokyo. It's a coffee shop by day, using beans roasted by the Fuglen team in nearby Kawasaki, and a cocktail bar by night. But there's a limited daytime cocktail menu too, and this spicy, flipped Manhattan is the highlight.

GLASSWARE: Coupe
GARNISH: Maraschino cherry

- ⅔ oz. | 20 ml rye whiskey
- 1⅓ oz. | 40 ml Chili-Infused Cinzano Rosso
- 1 dash Angostura Bitters

1. Combine all the ingredients in a mixing glass with ice, stir, and strain into a cocktail glass.

2. Garnish with the maraschino cherry.

CHILI-INFUSED CINZANO ROSSO: Slice two small chilies lengthwise and toast them in a dry pan. Place the toasted chilies in 1 liter of sweet vermouth and let steep for 2 hours. Strain before using or storing.

– BELLINI 95 –

THE BELLWOOD, SHIBUYA

This mashup of a Bellini and a French 95 is rich and nutty, and requires a serious amount of prep to get the texture and complexity just right. It's offered in an all-day café and bar run by Atsushi Suzuki, formerly of The SG Club and Shanghai's Sober Company. Suzuki wanted to recreate the atmosphere of the cafés that fostered Tokyo cocktail culture a century ago.

GLASSWARE: Champagne flute

- 2 oz. | 60 ml Bellini 95 Mix
- 2 oz. | 60 ml Champagne

1. Chill a champagne flute in the freezer.

2. Pour the chilled Bellini 95 Mix into the flute.

3. Add the Champagne and lift it once with a bar spoon.

BELLINI 95 MIX: Combine 200 ml Wakocha-Infused Whisky, 400 ml peach nectar, 200 ml cold-brew wakocha, 100 ml Pumpkin Seed Orgeat, 100 ml distilled water, and 80 ml fresh lemon juice. Add ⅓ tablespoon agar agar powder to 350 ml of the mixture (store what remains in the refrigerator,) stir to incorporate, and place in a pan. Warm over medium heat until the mixture starts to thicken, remove from heat, and refrigerate until the mixture is a light jelly, 2 to 3 hours. Strain before using or storing.

WAKOCHA-INFUSED WHISKY: Place 10 grams loose-leaf wakocha and 1 (750 ml) bottle of Dewar's 12 Year Old Whisky in a vacuum bag, seal it, and sous-vide at 125°F (52°C) for two hours. Strain before using or storing.

PUMPKIN SEED ORGEAT: Place 200 grams pumpkin seeds in a dry skillet and toast until lightly browned. Cover the seeds with water and let them soak overnight. Drain the seeds, place them in a blender, add 400 ml water, and puree until combined. Strain the mixture through a fine sieve or cheesecloth, add the liquid and 450 ml caster sugar to a bottle and stir until the sugar has dissolved. Stir in 30 ml of Bacardi Ocho and 3 drops orange blossom water and use or store in the refrigerator.

— HAVANA MARTINI —

MORI BAR GRAN, GINZA

In 1996, a customer asked Takao Mori, the Martini master (see page 34), to make him a Martini using rum. The guest had enjoyed one in another bar. Mori says he tried around 20 times before the customer said: "That's it!" Mori named it the Jamaica Martini at first, but after a study trip to Cuba in 2005, he settled on Havana Club 7-Year as the base and renamed the drink. It has become the second most popular cocktail in his bars.

GLASSWARE: Old Fashioned glass, stored in freezer
GARNISH: Olive

- 3 oz. | 90 ml Havana Club 7-Year Rum, stored in the freezer
- ½ teaspoon Valdespino Inocente Fino Sherry
- 1 drop orange bitters
- 1 strip of lemon peel

1. Add the rum, sherry, and bitters to a mixing glass containing large ice cubes. Stir briskly for 30 seconds.

2. Pour the cocktail into the chilled Old Fashioned glass, making sure to drop two of the ice cubes in the glass. Garnish with the olive, express the strip of lemon peel over the drink, and discard it.

— GIMLET HIGHBALL —

SANLUCAR BAR, KAGURAZAKA

Hard-shake inventor Kazuo Uyeda says only one other person has ever mastered his famous technique: his 20-year protégé Kiyoshi Shimbashi. For this daytime favorite, Shimbashi hard shakes a Gimlet with a touch more syrup than is standard, then tops it up with bubbles.

GLASSWARE: Highball glass

- 1½ oz. | 45 ml gin
- ½ oz. | 15 ml fresh lime juice
- 2 bar spoons simple syrup
- Club soda, to top

1. Combine all of the ingredients, except for the club soda, in a cocktail shaker filled with ice, hard shake, and strain into a highball glass filled with ice.

2. Top with the club soda.

– MYOUGA GIN & TONIC –

BAR ROCAILLE

Myouga is the pinkish brown bud, native to the Far East, that tastes like a piece of ginger kissed a citrus fruit. Hiromichi Itabashi uses it to great effect in this Gin & Tonic.

GLASSWARE: Highball glass
GARNISH: Myouga leaf

- 1 myouga bud
- 1 oz. | 30 ml Plymouth Gin
- 1 bar spoon fresh lime juice
- 3 oz. | 90 ml tonic water

1. Cut the myouga into pieces and place in a mixing glass.

2. Add the gin and juice and muddle well.

3. Strain into a highball glass, add two large ice cubes, and top with the tonic water.

— DOT LINE —

TIGRATO, YOTSUYA

Eight ingredients from eight countries across four continents, but it comes together beautifully for a rich, fruity, spicy cocktail that's good any time of day.

GLASSWARE: Old Fashioned glass

- ¼ oz. | 7 g Kenyan coffee, ground
- 1⅓ oz. | 40 ml Bacardi Carta Blanca rum
- ⅔ oz. | 20 ml umeshu
- 1 bar spoon Pedro Ximénez Sherry
- 1 bar spoon St-Germain
- 1 dash balsamic vinegar

1. Place a coffee dripper and a paper filter over a mixing glass and place the coffee in the filter.

2. Pour the rum, umeshu, sherry, and St-Germain over the coffee and let them drip into the glass.

3. Add the balsamic vinegar to the mixing glass, then ice, and stir to incorporate.

4. Strain into an Old Fashioned glass containing an ice sphere.

– YOKOTA –

CADIZ BAR, HAMAMATSUCHO

Masaru Yokota named his bar after the Spanish sherry province and has a fridge full of fortified wines. His passion caught the attention of sherry producer Lustau, who invited him to Jerez and asked him to create them a cocktail. It wasn't a perfect success: the sugar in Spain wasn't as sweet as he'd expected, and the lemons not as sour. But in his bar, with his ingredients, it's the perfect aperitif.

GLASSWARE: White wine glass

- 1 oz. | 30 ml Lustau Moscatel
- 2 bar spoons fresh lemon juice
- 2 bar spoons simple syrup
- Cava, to top

1. Combine all of the ingredients, except for the Cava, in a blender with crushed ice, pulse gently until the mixture turns into slush, and pour it into a glass.

2. Top with the Cava, using a spoon to lift it until thoroughly incorporated.

— SHERLOCK —

BAR SHERLOCK, GINZA

"In Japanese contests, the winning cocktails tend to be very sweet, but I wanted to make something sharper and more classic," says Takeshi Yoshimoto. He entered this into the Nippon Bartenders Association contest in 2013 and . . . didn't win. The following year he entered a sweeter drink and became national champion. But his first one is better. Don't skip the maraschino liqueur: Yoshimoto likens it to the binding ingredient in cooking.

GLASSWARE: Cocktail glass

- 1 oz. | 30 ml No. 3 London Dry Gin
- ½ oz. | 15 ml Mistia Muscat Liqueur
- 2 bar spoons Monin Green Banana Syrup
- 2 bar spoons fresh lime juice
- 1 bar spoon maraschino liqueur

1. Combine all of the ingredients with ice in a cocktail shaker, shake vigorously, and strain into a cocktail glass.

THE GIN BOOM

Japan's gin renaissance was perfectly timed. The whisky makers had shown that the country could be world-class at distilling, but they had become victims of their own success. Demand erupted in a manner nobody foresaw, inventory ran dry, and by 2015 even run-of-the-mill malts were selling at auction for silly prices.

Enter Japanese gin. In summer 2016, the country's first standalone gin distillery switched on its stills. The Kyoto Distillery was the brain-child of a duo that had helped create the Japanese whisky juggernaut. David Croll and Marcin Miller had taken leftover stock from the dismantled Karuizawa distillery and slowly built a following. In the early days, they had to give the whisky away. At the time of writing, bottles were changing hands for more than $150,000. As they drained their Karuizawa casks, they began wondering what to do next. "We did, briefly, consider opening a whisky distillery, but felt we would be jumping on a bandwagon and wanted to try something more pioneering," says Croll.

Japan had made gin before. Suntory launched Hermes Gin in 1936; Nikka began producing Gilbey's Gin under contract in the 1960s; and Asahi has been making Wilkinson Gin since 1995. But they all tasted British. It took some Brits to turn things Japanese. Croll and Miller hired distiller Alex Davies, formerly of Cotswolds Gin and Chase Gin in England, and they began scouring the Kyoto region for produce.

Around that time, a little bottle with a label that said only "Premium Japanese Craft Gin for Professional (sic)" began appearing in bars in Osaka. Bartenders were sworn to secrecy about the provenance, but would tell people it was made in Osaka by an established drinks company. That could only mean Suntory. The distilling giant was having another crack at gin, this time with more indigenous flavors. There were notes of sansho, shiso, and green tea. It was perhaps the first Japanese-tasting gin ever made, and it vanished as quietly as it had ap-

TOKYO COCKTAILS — 121

peared. It would be another three years before Suntory got it to market.

In that time, the Brits built a distillery from scratch, signed contracts with farmers, and slashed their way through a haystack of red tape. When their Ki No Bi Gin dropped, it made a big splash—a truly Japanese craft gin, using bamboo, yuzu, hinoki, gyokuro tea, shiso, and sansho among the botanicals. Davies distills in six flavor camps and then blends, which allows him to capture the peak of each ingredient more precisely, and means his employers can fire out new expressions at a furious pace. Navy strength, Old Tom, Karuizawa cask-aged, and an ultra-premium $500-a-pop bottle using prestige tea are among the releases to date.

If Croll thought the whisky boom was a bandwagon, he hadn't seen anything. In June 2017, Nikka Whisky released Coffey Gin, named after the Coffey still it's made in, with a strong sansho accent. Two months later, Suntory released Roku, with many, but not all, of the botanicals that had been in that mysterious little bottle. Soon enough, it seemed everyone with a still was making gin with local botanicals. It was quicker than making whisky, more lucrative than shochu, allowed for unlimited creativity, and made it easy to express a genuine sense of place in the bottle.

Ori-gin from Okinawa has aromas of pineapple and lemongrass on a base of local fire water awamori; Kozue, from umeshu specialists Nakano B.C., uses needles from the conifers growing around their local World Heritage site, Mount Koya. Sakurao gin from Hiroshima is made with shells from the local oyster industry. Benizakura, a dedicated gin distillery that opened in Hokkaido

in 2018, uses local kelp. And the makers of medicinal elixir Yomeishu released Ka No Mori, a gin they developed with Bar Orchard owners Takuo and Sumire Miyanohara (see page 148), flavored with 18 botanicals and the lindela wood that gives their elixir its distinctive taste.

At the most artisanal end of the spectrum sits Shohei Tatsumi, who makes Alchemiae Gin in the picturesque riverside town of Gujo Hachiman. Twice a month he releases a new style, around 600 bottles each time. One expression was a pure juniper gin, another had 61 different botanicals, and one used an oft-overlooked ingredient: giant water bug—two bugs' worth of flavor in every bottle. Tatsumi now has farmers asking him if it's possible to make gin with their produce. "I always just ask them to send it to me whenever it's at the peak of its fragrance," he says.

There are, at the time of writing, at least 30 producers and dozens of brands of Japanese gin, and unlike Japan's whisky industry, which took 80 years to command international attention, the gin folks are flying out of the gates.

WHERE TO DRINK JAPANESE GIN

BAR NAVEL, NAKANO
2-30-8 Nakano, Nakano-ku
In the off-piste Nakano neighborhood, Yuya Osawa runs a dusky, subterranean gin den with all the key Japanese names represented, plus dozens of imports.

TOKYO FAMILY RESTAURANT, SHIBUYA
1-3-1 Higashi, Shibuya-ku
This casual restaurant offers craft beers and 400 varieties of gin, around 50 of which come from Japan.

Spirits Bar Sunface, Shinjuku
10F, 1-13-7 Nishi Shinjuku, Shinjuku-ku
Owner Koji Esashi is known as a tequila man, but he's amassed one of the city's best gin collections.

Mixology Spirits Bang, Ginza
Plus Tokyo, 1-8-19, Ginza, Chuo-ku
Hidden inside the Plus Tokyo nightclub, Shuzo Nagumo's Japanese spirits bar is a good place to look for the rarest gins.

Cocktail Works Jinbocho, Jinbocho
3-7-13 Ogawamachi, Chiyoda-ku
The Cocktail Works chain has several outlets offering light mixology. This one also has around 180 brands of gin.

Kasumicho Bar Arashi
3-23-14 Nishi Azabu, Minato-ku
Chef-turned-bartender Hidekazu Takeda blends five Japanese gins and infuses them with tea, wasabi leaves, and a medley of other local ingredients to create his excellent Japanese G&T.

APERITIFS

CHARTREUSE MOJITO ✦ SHISUI ✦

NEGRONI ✦ BLACK NEGRONI ✦

WHISKY SOUR ✦ JFK ✦ I WISH I WAS

IN NEW ORLEANS ✦

GARDENING ORCHARD ✦ WISTERIA ✦

ORACIÓN ✦ TEA COCKTAIL ✦

GIN FIZZ ✦ OLD ENGLAND ✦

NEW-STYLE VERMOUTH COCKTAIL ✦

BLACK CAT ✦ SAPPORO ✦

PANTHEON ✦ HINOKI COCKTAIL ✦

OUGON NO TSUKI ✦ KING'S VALLEY ✦

RISING SUN

Tokyo's top preprandials, or the best ways to ease into an evening of drinking.

— CHARTREUSE MOJITO —

LE ZINC, SHINSEN

Yasuhiko Higuchi became interested in bartending after reading that his favorite designer, Takeo Kikuchi, liked Beefeater Gin. "I didn't know what it was, so I went to find some," he says. He loved it, and his passion was ignited. For seven years he studied with Kazuo Uyeda in Ginza, before opening Le Zinc, a bar designed to resemble the salon of a French boutique hotel. His true love these days is Chartreuse, but he says few Japanese people seem to share that passion.

GLASSWARE: Highball glass

- **1 bar spoon caster sugar**
- **Handful of fresh spearmint leaves**
- **1 lime wedge**
- **1 oz. | 30 ml Bacardi White Rum**
- **⅔ oz. | 20 ml Chartreuse Verte**
- **Club soda, to top**

1. Muddle the sugar and spearmint in a highball glass.

2. Squeeze the lime juice from the wedge into the glass, remove and discard the lime pulp, and place the wedge in the glass.

3. Add rum, Chartreuse, and cracked ice to the glass, top with soda, and muddle again until combined.

— SHISUI —

Akinori Shibuya won the 2018 Suntory Cocktail Competition with this drink, designed to taste *mizumizushii* (rough translation: "dewy and fresh"). It's a great prelude to a meal by Aileron owner and chef Kiyohachi Sato, who makes excellent retro sandwiches, omelets, and pasta dishes. Sato began bartending half a century ago at the Imperial Hotel, but long ago passed cocktail duty to Shibuya.

GLASSWARE: Cocktail glass

- ¾ oz. | 25 ml Suntory Roku Gin
- ½ oz. | 15 ml Mistia Muscat Liqueur
- 2 bar spoons fresh lemon juice
- 1 bar spoon Ginger Syrup
- 1 bar spoon matcha liqueur

1. Combine all of the ingredients with ice in a cocktail shaker, shake vigorously until chilled, and strain into a cocktail glass.

GINGER SYRUP: Add a peeled, 1-inch piece of ginger to a standard simple syrup after the sugar has dissolved and cook for another 5 minutes. Let cool, strain, and store in an airtight container.

NEGRONI

The popular game show *TV Champion* ran for 14 years on Japanese television. Every Thursday, contestants would go head-to-head in such esoteric pursuits as Styrofoam sculpting, excavator dexterity, or furniture removal. It was a 1993 episode about cocktails and ice-ball carving that inspired a 16-year-old Daisuke Fujita to become a bartender, though the whizz! bang! splat! production style of the show couldn't be further removed from what he does now.

Fujita makes classic cocktails and serves them in stunning antique glassware—most of it hand-carried home from Europe, some of it dating back to the 19th century. His bar, designed to resemble the drawing room of a Piedmont villa, is crammed with Romano Levi grappas and whiskies so rare you probably shouldn't drink them.

His cocktails often contain blends of gins or whiskies or liqueurs or bitters. "It would be best if there were single bottles with the profile I want," he says. "But if not, I'll get the balance by mixing them."

So, for his standout Negroni he combines the gins Tanqueray No. Ten and Gordon's. The former is fruity and sharp but too gentle, he says, and the latter has the juniper punch but is too heavy on its own. Then he mixes Carpano Antica Formula Vermouth with the lighter Punto e Mes from the same maker. Antica Formula is rich, with cinnamon notes, but it lacks sharpness; Punt e Mes is a little more bitter, but not solid enough, he says.

Instead of building the drink over ice, he swirls the ingredients in a brandy snifter, then pours it into the glass. That way, he only needs a short stir to create what is a fantastically complex Negroni.

And he recommends skipping the traditional orange peel. It looks nice, he says, but in terms of flavor "it's too much."

GLASSWARE: Old Fashioned glass

- 1 bar spoon Punt e Mes Sweet Vermouth, plus more to rinse
- 1 oz. | 30 ml Tanqueray No. Ten Gin
- 2 bar spoons Gordon's London Dry Gin
- 2 bar spoons Campari
- 1 bar spoon Carpano Antica Formula Sweet Vermouth
- 3 drops Abbott's Bitters

1. Place an ice cube in an Old Fashioned glass and pour a little Punt e Mes vermouth over it, then strain.

2. Add all the ingredients to a wine glass or brandy snifter and swirl.

3. Pour the cocktail from a height into the Old Fashioned glass.

4. Stir briefly and serve.

— BLACK NEGRONI —

Hidetsugu Ueno had just returned from Milan and a visit to the Fernet-Branca distillery when Gary Regan asked him to contribute a recipe to his book, *The Negroni*. Ueno had seen plenty of white Negronis, but never a black one, so he came up with this potent aperitif.

GLASSWARE: Old Fashioned glass
GARNISH: Strip of lemon peel

- 1½ oz. | 45 ml gin
- 1 oz. | 30 ml Carpano Antica Formula Sweet Vermouth
- ½ oz. | 15 ml Fernet-Branca

1. Build the cocktail in an Old Fashioned glass containing one large ice cube and stir to combine.

2. Express the strip of lemon peel over the drink and then place the peel on the rim of the glass.

— WHISKY SOUR —

BAR LANDSCAPE, GINZA

In 2013, Kazuma Matsuo won top prize in the annual Nippon Bartenders Association cocktail contest. For a classic Japanese bartender, that's a Palme d'Or, a Pritzker Prize, a Man Booker—the best you can do on the national stage, and a guarantee that people will follow your career. Three years later, his wife Tamiko won the same trophy. So when they announced they were opening a bar together, it had people chattering.

Bar Landscape debuted in the spring of 2019, directly opposite the bar of Tamiko's first mentor, Takao Mori, and 20 feet from Kazuma's previous home, the storied Little Smith. Their different lineages mean Landscape has two distinct house styles for most drinks, with different tools, different techniques, and different base spirits. You can see it in the Martinis, you can see it in the Gimlets, but you see it most clearly in the Whisky Sours.

The simple way to say it is that Kazuma makes foreign-style whisky sours, using egg white, because Little Smith—a cinematically beautiful subterranean hollow—was popular with foreign visitors. Tamiko makes them in the classic, egg-free way because her former bars Blossom and OPA rarely saw foreign visitors, and on the rare occasion a Japanese drinker asks for a Whisky Sour, they're not expecting protein.

KAZUMA MATSUO WHISKY SOUR

"I think egg white creates more depth," says Kazuma Matsuo, who pairs Johnnie Walker Black with one of its key malts.

GLASSWARE: Sour glass

- ⅔ oz. | 20 ml fresh lemon juice
- 2 bar spoons caster sugar
- 1¼ oz. | 35 ml Johnnie Walker Black Label Scotch Whisky
- 2 bar spoons Talisker 10 Year Old Scotch Whisky
- 2 bar spoons egg white
- 3 drops Angostura Bitters

1. Combine the lemon and sugar in a cocktail shaker and stir until the sugar has dissolved, then add the whiskies.

2. Froth the egg white, add it to the shaker, and then add ice. Shake vigorously and strain into the sour glass.

3. Top with the bitters.

TAMIKO MATSUO WHISKY SOUR

"If you chill it too much it kills the aroma," says Tamiko Matsuo, who swirls and throws to mix and aerate the cocktail before adding ice for a short shake.

GLASSWARE: Sour glass

GARNISH: 1 strip of lemon peel studded with cloves

- 1½ oz. | 45 ml Dewar's 12 Year Old Scotch Whisky
- ⅔ oz. | 20 ml fresh lemon juice
- 1 tablespoon caster sugar
- 2 bar spoons fresh orange juice
- 3 drops Angostura Bitters

1. Combine the whisky and lemon juice in a wine glass; taste and adjust if necessary.

2. Add sugar and swirl the glass, then add the orange juice and swirl again until thoroughly mixed.

3. Throw the liquid from the glass into a cocktail shaker, pour it back into the glass, and throw again; repeat until the aroma of the orange juice emerges.

4. Shake with four small ice cubes and then strain into the sour glass.

5. Top with the bitters and garnish with the clove-studded strip of lemon peel.

— JFK —

BAR HOSHI, GINZA

Like a Martini or an Alaska, this is a pre-dinner drink with a punch. It's a liquid tribute to Yuichi Hoshi's favorite US president, who reportedly had an appetite for Tanqueray. The pimento-stuffed olive is a nod to the gin bottle: all green with a little red dot.

GLASSWARE: Cocktail glass

GARNISH: Pimento-stuffed olive

- 1½ oz. | 45 ml Tanqueray No. Ten Gin
- 2 bar spoons Grand Marnier
- 2 bar spoons dry sherry (Hoshi uses Williams & Humbert's Don Zoilo Fino)
- 2 dashes orange bitters
- 1 strip of orange peel, for flaming

1. Combine all of the ingredients, except for the orange peel, in a mixing glass with ice, stir until chilled, and strain into a cocktail glass.

2. Flame the strip of orange peel over the glass and garnish with the olive.

— I WISH I WAS IN NEW ORLEANS —

BAR QWANG, NISHI AZABU

Yasuhiro Hasegawa makes the cocktails at Qwang; his wife Junko makes Thai dishes to match them. This cousin of the French 75 suits the deep-fried spring rolls with fish sauce and plum.

GLASSWARE: Champagne flute

GARNISH: Lemon peel

- ⅔ oz. | 20 ml Havana Club 7-Year Rum
- ⅓ oz. | 20 ml Giffard Wild Elderflower Liqueur
- 1¼ teaspoons | 7 ml fresh lime juice
- 2 dashes Peychaud's Bitters
- Brut Champagne, to top

1. Combine all of the ingredients, except the Champagne, with ice in a cocktail shaker, shake vigorously, and strain into the flute.

2. Top with Champagne and garnish with lemon peel.

When husband-and-wife bartenders Takuo and Sumire Miyahohara moved from Nara to Tokyo and opened Bar Orchard in 2008 on the elite street Sotobori Dori, they heard a few grumbles from their early visitors. "They said what we were doing wasn't Ginza style," says Takuo. The critics were displeased to see saline foam, crispy bacon garnishes, and liquid nitrogen on their most hallowed cocktail turf. And then there's the presentation. Some drinks come in cocktail glasses, but others arrive in plastic bathtubs, miniature garbage cans, egg cartons, or baby bottles. The detractors were in the minority though, and were missing the point. Bar Orchard is a fun place to have serious cocktails. They make Manhattans and Mock Manhattans (see page 333) with equal aplomb. And 12 years after those early grumbles, the couple had to install a doorbell entry system to help them handle the swarms of people looking to enter.

— GARDENING ORCHARD —

BAR ORCHARD, GINZA

It's citrusy, refreshing, beautifully balanced, and it comes with a watering can of absinthe on the side. As you sip, you sprinkle the green fairy to your taste.

GLASSWARE: Miniature bucket

GARNISH: Bean sprout, matcha powder, and cinnamon

- 1 yuzu wedge
- 1 shiso leaf
- 1½ oz. | 45 ml Ka No Mori Gin
- 2 bar spoons yuzu liqueur
- 2 bar spoons white wine
- 2 bar spoons fresh lemon juice
- 2 bar spoons simple syrup
- 1 bay leaf, toasted
- Absinthe, to taste

1. Squeeze the juice of the yuzu wedge into a Boston shaker and throw in the spent wedge. Tear the shiso leaf and add it to the shaker. Add the gin, liqueur, wine, lemon juice, and simple syrup and muddle.

2. Add a small scoop of crushed ice to the shaker, shake vigorously, and pour into the bucket. Add more crushed ice and a straw and garnish with the bean sprout. Sprinkle the matcha powder and cinnamon over the cocktail.

3. Place the bay leaf in a miniature watering can, pour light absinthe over it, and serve alongside the cocktail.

— WISTERIA —

GASLIGHT EVE, GINZA

Naomi Takahashi took an analytical approach to her shot at a world title. She was heading to Prague in 2013 to represent Japan in the Before Dinner category at the IBA world championships. She studied winning recipes from previous years and saw that the international judges seemed to have sweeter palates than their Japanese counterparts, and appeared to award stirred drinks more than shaken. She crunched the data and came up with a stirred drink that starts sweet and turns gradually dry. And she won.

GLASSWARE: Cocktail glass

- 1⅓ oz. | 40 ml Havana Club 3-Year Rum
- ½ oz. | 15 ml Mistica Muscat Liqueur
- 2 bar spoons dry vermouth
- 1 bar spoon Grand Marnier

1. Combine the ingredients with ice in a mixing glass, stir until chilled, and strain into the cocktail glass.

– ORACÍÓN –

H ere's a cocktail packed with tonics and restoratives by Asami Saito, who lived the apple-a-day life as the daughter of apple farmers. There's lime to fight scurvy, apricot for antioxidants, and sage with antimicrobial properties. Absinthe is the multipurpose elixir. And the rum refers to the tenuous tale that doctors cured Spanish King Alfonso XII's flu by getting him to drink a bottle of Bacardi.

GLASSWARE: Champagne flute

GARNISH: Fresh sage leaves

- 1⅔ oz. | 50 ml Bacardi Reserva Ocho rum
- 1½ oz. | 45 ml apple juice
- ½ oz. | 15 ml fresh lime juice
- 2 bar spoons apricot jam
- 2 dashes absinthe
- 1 oz. | 30 ml sparkling wine

1. Combine all the ingredients, except for the sparkling wine, in a cocktail shaker containing ice, shake vigorously, and strain into a Champagne flute.

2. Top with the sparkling wine and attach the sage leaves to the glass stem for their aroma.

— TEA COCKTAIL —

SUKIYABASHI SAMBOA, GINZA

*S*amboa bars—there are three in Tokyo and 11 elsewhere in Japan—are so famous for their highballs that Atsushi Tsuda, who runs the Sukiyabashi branch, says there are days he never even picks up a shaker. But his regulars know that his true masterpiece is this shaken cocktail featuring his favorite gin, which he infuses with an extra helping of the key botanicals.

GLASSWARE: Cocktail glass

GARNISH: Strip of lime peel

- 1¼ oz. | 35 ml Herb-Infused Tanqueray No. Ten
- ½ oz. | 15 ml Mistica Muscat Liqueur
- 2 bar spoons Fauchon Tea Liqueur
- 1 bar spoon fresh lemon juice

1. Combine all the ingredients with ice in a cocktail shaker, shake vigorously, and strain into a cocktail glass. Garnish with the strip of lime peel.

HERB-INFUSED TANQUERAY NO. TEN: Take a fistful of herbs—50 percent chamomile and 50 percent a mix of peppermint, cardamom, and lemongrass—and add it to 1 (750 ml) bottle of Tanqueray No. Ten. Let steep for 6 hours and strain before using or storing.

— GIN FIZZ —

Bar Dolphy is a sepia-toned basement bar where the music isn't *always* Eric Dolphy, but it's never far off. Bartender Ryosaku Yamaura runs it solo and makes classics in the most unhurried style imaginable. "It may be Galapagos thinking," he says, "but a bartender should devote themselves to each customer, one drink at a time, and take exactly as long as they need."

It's hard to pinpoint why his Gin Fizz is so good. Perhaps it's because he squeezes the juice after you order the drink. The gin is critical, of course. Yamaura says Beefeater is best when you're pairing with lemon juice, and the gin has to be chilled to -4°F (-20°C). He says even at 5°F (-15°C) the spirit will be too loose. Like most of his Tokyo peers, he rinses his hand-cut ice before use. Unusually, he rinses it with club soda when he's making a gin fizz. He reasons that it's better to use the liquid he'll be mixing with. This isn't a place for small economies. And his shake is distinctive: an almost vertical thrust, something like the motion you'd use when pumping up a bicycle tire.

What you get for all his trouble is a benchmark Gin Fizz with perfectly balanced sweetness and acidity.

- 1½ oz. | 45 ml Beefeater Gin (94 proof), stored in the freezer
- ½ oz. | 15 ml fresh lemon juice
- 2 bar spoons caster sugar, plus more as needed
- Club soda, as needed

1. Place the gin, the lemon juice, and the sugar in a cobbler shaker and stir vigorously with a spoon. Taste the mixture; it should taste like sour lemon candy. If it doesn't, add more sugar or lemon juice as needed.

2. Place hand-cut ice cubes in a glass, rinse with soda, and strain.

3. Add ice to the shaker, shake vigorously, and double-strain into the highball glass.

4. Top with club soda until the glass is three-quarters full. Hook the spoon under the ice cubes and lift; don't stir.

5. Fold a square of lemon peel over the glass and press down—do not twist—on the rim on the part of the glass furthest from the guest's mouth. It's for their nose, not their tongue.

— OLD ENGLAND —

LUPIN, GINZA

Lupin, in business since 1928, once had the good fortune to be located next to publishing house Bungei Shunju, which supplied them with hard-drinking authors and artists. Osamu Dazai, Ango Sakaguchi, and Taro Okamoto were among the patrons, and the only change since their day is that the walls are a deeper shade of orange. Current head bartender Ikuo Hiraki has been mixing drinks since the early 1970s. Ask him for a short, dry cocktail and he'll often suggest an Old England, a simple, long-forgotten recipe that he thinks should be revived. He suggests Lustau's nutty La Ina Fino for the sherry.

GLASSWARE: Chilled cocktail glass

- 1 oz. | 30 ml Fino sherry
- 1 oz. | 30 ml vodka

1. Combine the sherry and vodka in a mixing glass with ice, stir, and strain into the chilled glass.

— NEW-STYLE —
VERMOUTH COCKTAIL

BAR ANTHEM, GINZA

Bar Anthem has a cabinet crammed with rare cocktail books. One fragile Japanese work from the start of the 20th century features a curious, confusing recipe that uses the measurements "wahai" and "youhai." That translates as "Japanese cup" and "Western cup," but no living person seems to know what those terms mean.

A New-Style Vermouth Cocktail requires a Western cup of vermouth, two Japanese cups of maraschino liqueur, two Japanese cups of Angostura Bitters, the peel of a lemon, slices of lemon, and an unspecified amount of gum syrup. The method was so vague it was almost useless, but it did say that you should muddle the lemon peel in the vermouth.

Anthem owner Atsushi Asakura explained that old Japanese cocktail books were often vague and frequently contained mistakes because publishing houses saw them as easy money, hired second-rate writers, and churned the books out. *Plus ça change* . . .

In deciphering the recipe, we began by assuming that the measurements were based on a jigger, with 45 milliliters of dry vermouth, and 30 each of maraschino liqueur and Angostura Bitters. Where the recipe said "peel of lemon," Asakura used the peel of a whole fruit. The result was rich, bitter, aromatic, invigorating, and delicious. Like an aperitif Manhattan for the fearless. Case closed. I thought.

The next time I visited, Asakura had reassessed the recipe, increasing the vermouth and bringing the liqueur and bitters down to a more moderate 10 milliliters each. It was more elegant, and even better.

Then he asked for time to research a more definitive answer. The next time we met, he postulated that it might be similar to the traditional Vermouth Cocktail, with just dashes of maraschino liqueur and Angostura.

That was nice enough, better for a bartender's profit margin, and more plausible in all respects but one: Could a "Japanese cup" really have meant a dash?

NEW-STYLE VERMOUTH COCKTAIL A

GLASSWARE: Coupe

- Peel of 1 lemon
- 2 oz. | 60 ml dry vermouth
- 2 bar spoons maraschino liqueur
- 2 bar spoons Angostura Bitters
- 1 bar spoon simple syrup
- 3 lemon slices

1. Place the lemon peel and vermouth in a mixing glass and muddle.

2. Combine the vermouth and the remaining ingredients with ice in a mixing glass, stir until chilled, and strain into a coupe.

NEW-STYLE VERMOUTH COCKTAIL B

GLASSWARE: Coupe

- 1 strip of lemon peel
- 2 oz. | 60 ml dry vermouth
- 2 dashes maraschino liqueur
- 2 dashes Angostura Bitters
- 3 lemon slices
- simple syrup, to taste

1. Place the lemon peel and vermouth in a mixing glass and muddle.

2. Combine the vermouth and the remaining ingredients with ice in a mixing glass, stir, and strain into a coupe.

— BLACK CAT —

Yomeishu is made in Nagano prefecture, where Yasuhiko Mizusawa grew up drinking it. The bittersweet herbal elixir is sold in drugstores as a remedy for fatigue, poor circulation, and gastrointestinal issues. That branding is why most bartenders ignore it, but the former Nippon Bartenders Association champion pairs it brilliantly with a whisky that also hails from Nagano prefecture.

GLASSWARE: Old Fashioned glass
GARNISH: Strip of orange peel

- 1 oz. | 30 ml Mars Iwai Tradition Whisky
- ½ oz. | 15 ml Yomeishu
- ½ oz. | 15 ml white peach liqueur
- 1 bar spoon fresh lemon juice

1. Combine the ingredients with ice in a two-piece cocktail shaker, shake very briefly, and strain over ice into an Old Fashioned glass.

— SAPPORO —

BAR STING, SHINJUKU

When the city of Sapporo was gearing up to host the 1972 Winter Olympics, its most famous bartender created a cocktail for the occasion. Tatsuro Yamazaki ran Bar Yamazaki from 1958 until his death in 2016 at the age of 96, and his contribution to cocktail culture earned him an Order of the Rising Sun medal from the Emperor. In Tokyo, Atsushi Fukasawa still serves the Sapporo in his stylish Bar Sting, a hideaway furnished in Frank Lloyd Wright and Le Corbusier designs.

GLASSWARE: Cocktail glass

GARNISH: Green cocktail cherry

- 1 oz. | 30 ml vodka
- 2 bar spoons amaretto
- 2 bar spoons Chartreuse Verte
- 2 bar spoons dry vermouth

1. Combine all the ingredients in a mixing glass with ice, strain into a cocktail glass, and garnish with the cherry.

— PANTHEON —

LAND BAR ARTISAN, SHINBASHI

You can file this under whisky drinks, but Daisuke Ito sees it as Bénédictine modified with Scotch and lemon juice. He designed it to showcase a liqueur that he believes is woefully underrated. Don't hesitate to experiment with various whiskies—Ito says it works with all kinds of Scotch.

GLASSWARE: Cocktail glass

- 1 oz. | 30 ml Scotch whisky
- ½ oz. | 15 ml Bénédictine
- ½ oz. | 15 ml fresh lemon juice

1. Combine all of the ingredients with ice in a cocktail shaker, shake vigorously, and strain into a cocktail glass.

Daisuke Ito is perhaps Tokyo's staunchest defender of classic cocktails. "Nobody orders a *fun* cocktail twice," he says, and goes on to compare his drinks to a mom's cooking, drawing on a long heritage of vernacular recipes and techniques to create something reassuringly familiar.

He got serious about bartending after serving his first professional Gimlet in his home city of Sendai. It was a flop. "The customer was nice about it, but he said it didn't taste like the Gimlets in Ginza," Ito says. So the following day he took a five-hour bus ride to Ginza, and, with a cocktail magazine as his guide, toured the district comparing Gimlets.

"I didn't go to Uyeda-san's bar (see page 39), but there was one Gimlet that stood out," he recalls. That was in Star Bar Ginza and was made by head bartender Hidetsugu Ueno, now proprietor of Bar High Five. Ito asked for advice, and Star Bar owner Hisashi Kishi offered him an apprenticeship. He spent eight years training with Kishi and Ueno before going independent in 2014.

– HINOKI COCKTAIL –

BAR LIQUID RUBY, SHINJUKU

One sip of Laphroaig convinced Naotaka Mukaiyama to quit his job in Japan's Self-Defense Forces and turn to whisky. He took work in a Shinjuku-area whisky bar, then moved to Spirits Bar Sunface (see page 125), before opening the bourbon-focused Bar Liquid Ruby in 2019. His riff on a Whisky Sour is accented with *hinoki* (Japanese cypress) and served in a *masu* (cypress sake box).

GLASSWARE: Cypress sake masu

- 1⅓ oz. | 40 ml Yamazaki whisky
- ½ oz. | 15 ml fresh lemon juice
- ⅓ oz. | 10 ml Hinoki Syrup
- 1 egg white
- 5 drops The Japanese Bitters Hinoki Bitters

1. Blend all ingredients with a hand mixer.

2. Combine with ice in a Boston shaker and shake well.

3. Strain into the masu.

HINOKI SYRUP: Place hinoki wood chips and equal parts sugar and water in a saucepan. Bring to a boil, lower heat, and reduce until syrupy. Strain and store.

— OUGON NO TSUKI —

BAR RADIO, AOYAMA

Koji Ozaki's *The Bar Radio Cocktail Book* is the most beautiful, comprehensive publication of its kind, with 1,188 recipes, both standard and original. One drink it does not feature is the Ougon no Tsuki ("Golden Moon"), which Ozaki created in 2008 for a *Japan Times* feature on summer cocktails. Ozaki now lives in Kyoto and makes only sporadic appearances at Bar Radio, so if you wish to try this, best make it yourself.

GLASSWARE: Cocktail glass

- 1½ oz. | 45 ml London Dry gin
- 1 oz. | 30 ml fresh lemon juice
- 2 bar spoons caster sugar
- 1 egg yolk

1. Place the ingredients in a cocktail shaker and whisk to combine.

2. Add ice to the shaker, shake briefly, and strain into the cocktail glass.

— KING'S VALLEY —

Kazuo Uyeda makes Sidecars, White Ladies, and Silent Thirds with ratios that emphasize the spirit, and this cocktail from the same family is no exception. He says of all the recipes he has devised in his long career, this is his favorite, invented in 1986 for a Scotch whisky contest. He won, of course.

GLASSWARE: Cocktail glass

- 1⅓ oz. | 40 ml blended Scotch whisky
- 2 bar spoons Cointreau
- 2 bar spoons fresh lime juice
- 1 bar spoon blue Curaçao

1. Combine all the ingredients with ice in a cocktail shaker, hard shake (see page 39), and strain into a cocktail glass.

THE ORIGINAL MR. MARTINI

*"It only takes 10 years to learn technique.
What you really need to learn is hospitality."*
KIYOSHI IMAI, AS TOLD BY HIROYUKI MIURA

Takao Mori (see page 34) isn't the first Martini King of Tokyo. That was
Kiyoshi Imai, chief bartender at the Palace Hotel's Royal Bar. From the
1950s until his retirement in 1984, Imai was so famous for the drink

that many people of the era knew him only as "Mr. Martini", and his method has influenced every top Tokyo bartender since.

Imai was a country boy, raised in a coastal village 400 kilometers west of Tokyo. He was hoping to become a train driver but life took a turn when his elder sister moved to Yokohama and became neighbors with one of the most famous bartenders of the era. Haruyoshi Honda had built his reputation bartending at the Grand Hotel and Imperial Hotel. In the 1930s he was running the bar at an elite drinking and dining complex called the Tokyo Kaikan and he offered the young boy a job.

Imai was 15 when he headed to Tokyo, and 17 when the war put the brakes on his career. He was sent to work in a steel mill, then enlisted in the army. It was four years before he rejoined Honda at the Kaikan, and this time the job was very different. Japan was under occupation and alcohol had been criminalized. The only people who could enjoy cocktails were the occupying forces, who had commandeered the Kaikan and were drinking with vigor and teaching the bartenders about drinks back home. They also held rooftop parties with live jazz bands and Imai, in his early 20s at this point, was captivated by the musicians. He later told people that his distinctive horizontal swing shake was based on the way the percussionists shook their maracas.

According to biographer Koichi Edagawa, Imai slept on a makeshift bed inside the bar, partly because there was no time to go home, and partly because the place had become a target for liquor thieves. One night, he fled an armed raid.

The alcohol ban was lifted in 1949, and the Americans gave the Kaikan back, but the bar remained an elite space, out of reach of the average office worker. It was in this period that Imai started working on his Martini.

Initially, he struggled with the stir. It was either watery from too much stirring, or too warm for the opposite reason. Then, one evening, a customer took him to a bar in Ginza where the owner poured him a glass of ice-cold gin. It was his eureka moment. He went straight back to the bar, put a bottle of Gordon's on ice, and soon had the method that would make him famous.

At the end of the 1950s, developers were planning a new luxury landmark called the Palace Hotel and they hired Imai to run the bar. The Kaikan clientele followed him, and in came high-rolling international travelers.

"It was known as the place to go for the latest drinks," says Hiroyuki Miura, who worked under Imai for nine years and went on to helm the bar himself. "The liquor was always more up-to-date than anywhere else. Our guests traveled a lot. They would come back and talk about something they'd tried, and maybe bring a gift. One time it was a box of limes, a bottle of cachaça, and an explanation of Caipirinhas."

Miura says bartenders were mostly treated as servants at the time, but Imai was different. "I could see the respect he commanded from people," he says. "Imai-san was like a Buddha, always smiling, listening more than he spoke, and he was a master of hospitality."

Imai's Bloody Mary became famous. He would give the guests vodka, tomato juice, and all the condiments separately and tell them to build it themselves. He made a distinctive Sidecar by throwing an orange slice in the shaker. But it was his Martini that became legendary. Miura can't say exactly why, because as the protégé he was never allowed to try one. "Other hotels' bartenders often came here to drink," he says. "But I couldn't." He watched carefully though, and says it involved a chilled 94-proof Gordon's Gin, more vermouth than modern drinkers would expect, no bitters, a beautiful stir in a custom-made extra-thick mixing glass, and a twist of lemon.

Imai died in January 1999 at the age of 74, but his legacy lives on in many ways. He created the Hotel Bartenders Association; he was a mentor to many great bartenders, including Kazuo Uyeda (see page 39) and Fumihiko Kimura (see page 315); and if you order a Martini in any top Tokyo bar now, the bartender will reach into the fridge or freezer for the gin.

— RISING SUN —

In the 1960s, the Ministry of Health, Labor and Welfare was inexplicably sponsoring cocktail contests, and the '63 prize went to this patriotic number by tequila fan Kiyoshi Imai. He didn't have access to fresh limes when he was bartending, which is just as well because this recipe only works with the sweetened stuff from a bottle. It is an exceptional cocktail, rolling with waves of flavor.

GLASSWARE: Coupe

- Salt, for the rim
- 1 maraschino cherry
- 1½ oz. | 45 ml silver tequila
- ⅔ oz. | 20 ml Chartreuse Jaune
- ½ oz. | 15 ml lime cordial
- 1 bar spoon sloe gin

1. Rim a coupe with the salt and place the cherry in the bottom of the glass.

2. Add the tequila, Chartreuse, and lime cordial to a cocktail shaker with ice, shake vigorously, and strain into the glass. Add the sloe gin on top and it will sink through the cocktail.

FRESH FRUIT
COCKTAILS

APPLE COCKTAIL +

KIWI ABSINTHE GIMLET +

KYOHO & EARL GREY MARTINI +

PLUM COCKTAIL +

YUZU MATCHA MARTINI +

BLOOD RED DIAMOND

In a city that can charge $10 for a perfect peach and $200 for a musk melon, it's no small luxury to drink a fresh fruit cocktail. It's also in line with the philosophy underpinning Tokyo's best culinary experiences: seasonality.

Want a Bellini? Come in July or August when peaches are in season. No serious Tokyo bartender will pour juice from a carton, or use a peach that's been held in cold storage out of season.

Shinobu Ishigaki of the bar Ishinohana says even knowing what's in season isn't enough. "You have to understand the arc of the season," he says. "The way you use a fruit early in its season is quite different from how you use the same fruit at the peak of its power."

The rise of the fresh fruit cocktail in Tokyo coincided with two phenomena: the increase in female guests and the importing of quality fresh fruit.

In the 1960s, even a lime cost several times more than most people would pay for a drink. By the 1980s, fruit was flying in from elsewhere in Asia, the Americas, and Europe. From the 1990s it became common to have a fruit bowl on display as a signal that this was a place of luxuries.

Japanese bartenders source fruit in much the same way chefs get their fish. They hire professional buyers to visit a morning market, the

largest of which is Ota Wholesale Market near Haneda airport, where they handle close to a million tons of produce a day. At 6:50 a.m., bidding begins for the top-grade produce. Yasuhiko Mizusawa of Bar Tiare in Akasaka says he will only consider Grade A fruit. "Grade B goes to supermarkets," he says. "It's not delicious."

Mizusawa, who penned a book about fresh fruit cocktails in 2011, has a binder of notes detailing peak seasons, provenance, flavor profiles, and usage ideas. He says these drinks are a way for people to feel the changing of the seasons, and for those who have migrated to the big city to get a taste of their hometowns.

— APPLE COCKTAIL —

BAR TIARE, ASAKUSA

Half naughty, half healthy. You need an apple that's sweet and a little soft, says Yasuhiko Mizusawa. He favors the Fuji variety and may keep the fruit a day or two to let it soften. The syrup is made from karintou, an old-school snack of fried dough in brown sugar. Substitute simple syrup made with brown sugar.

GLASSWARE: Old Fashioned glass

GARNISH: Apple slice

- 1½ oz. | 45 ml vodka
- ¼ apple
- 1½ teaspoons | 7.5 ml karintou or brown sugar syrup
- 1 bar spoon minced fresh ginger
- 1 bar spoon fresh lemon juice
- Ginger ale, to top

1. Place all of the ingredients, except for the ginger ale, in a blender and puree until smooth.

2. Pour over ice into an Old Fashioned glass, top with the ginger ale, and garnish with the apple slice.

— KIWI ABSINTHE GIMLET —

BAR CIELO, SANGENJAYA

"I thought the green notes of kiwi might suit absinthe," says Hiroyuki Hieda, a Ginza-trained barman who runs a two-tier space in bohemian Sangenjaya. The lower level is the informal "botanical bar," where craft gin has the spotlight. Upstairs, in the "authentic bar," the fresh-fruit cocktails are the stars.

GLASSWARE: Cocktail glass

- 1 kiwi
- 1⅕ oz. | 35 ml gin (Hieda uses a blend of Tanqueray and Bobby's)
- ½ oz. | 15 ml absinthe
- 1 bar spoon fresh lime juice
- 1 bar spoon simple syrup

1. Juice the kiwi, straining the liquid through cheesecloth.

2. Add the juice and the remaining ingredients, along with ice, to a cocktail shaker, shake vigorously, and strain into a cocktail glass.

— KYOHO & EARL GREY MARTINI —

ROYAL BAR, PALACE HOTEL TOKYO, OTEMACHI

Manabu Ohtake beat 10,000 other contestants to win the Diageo World Class contest in 2011, and was quickly tapped by the Palace Hotel Tokyo to helm their historic, moodily lit Royal Bar. Each month he introduces new cocktails, usually based around fresh fruit. Autumn is the season for sweet Kyoho grapes, which he shakes with Earl Grey leaves for a beautiful bergamot accent.

GLASSWARE: Cocktail glass

GARNISH: Kyoho grape

- 1⅓ oz. | 40 ml CÎROC Vodka
- 7 to 8 Kyoho grapes
- 1 bar spoon loose-leaf Earl Grey tea

1. Add all of the ingredients to a cocktail shaker and muddle.

2. Add ice, shake vigorously, and strain into the chilled glass. Garnish with an additional grape.

— PLUM COCKTAIL —

YANAGIKOJI BAR MARUUME, FUTAKO TAMAGAWA

The upmarket Futako Tamagawa suburb is home to a stunning bar in a converted wooden warehouse that looks as though it were plucked from the streets of Kyoto.

Bartender Takashi Makishima, who actually was plucked from the old capital, makes classics and hyper-seasonal fruit cocktails. This one, with a lush texture and long finish, is on the menu from late May to late June.

GLASSWARE: Cocktail glass

- 2 sumomo plums*
- 1 oz. | 30 ml Tanqueray Gin
- 1 oz. | 30 ml cranberry juice
- 1 bar spoon grenadine

1. Juice the plums, straining the liquid through cheesecloth.

2. Add the plum juice and the remaining ingredients to a Boston shaker with ice, shake vigorously, and strain into a cocktail glass.

Sumomo, or prunus salicina, are usually sold as Japanese plums, Chinese plums, or Asian plums in English-speaking countries.

— YUZU MATCHA MARTINI —

BAR ISHINOHANA, SHIBUYA

Grilled zest and a splash of juice is all it takes to tell your senses that this is a yuzu drink.

GLASSWARE: Cocktail glass
GARNISH: 1 strip of grilled yuzu zest

- 1½ oz. | 45 ml vodka
- 1 oz. | 30 ml fresh grapefruit juice
- 1 bar spoon fresh yuzu juice
- 1 bar spoon matcha powder

1. Add all of the ingredients to a cocktail shaker with ice, shake vigorously, and strain into a cocktail glass.

2. Garnish with the strip of grilled yuzu zest.

ISHINOHANA

Shinobu Ishigaki served his apprenticeship on the customer side of the counter. He would enter any door with the sign "Bar" above it, order one cocktail—always a Sidecar—and leave. "I could only afford one drink in each place, and the Sidecar recipe is unforgiving, so I could watch the technique and taste the outcome," he says.

In Tokyo, where lineage matters, being a self-taught bartender is like being a pilot who learned to fly by watching *Top Gun*, but Ishigaki sees it as a blessing that freed him to find a style of his own.

He developed an innovative streak while working in a sukiyaki restaurant. His job was to create cocktails to match the dishes—an ume-shiso daiquiri paired with grilled saury, for example—and because the food menu changed fast, so did his cocktails.

He was still there when he won the Nippon Bartenders Association contest with a drink called Polar Star (1$\frac{1}{3}$ oz. aquavit, $\frac{1}{3}$ oz. apple syrup, $\frac{1}{3}$ oz. fresh lemon juice; shake). National champions rarely wait long to start their own bars and Ishigaki was no exception. He opened Ishinohana the following year and almost immediately added to his trophy cabinet with top prize in an international contest, the Bacardi Martini Grand Prix. There was a big buzz locally; then Anthony Bourdain made it global by featuring Ishinohana on his *No Reservations* TV series.

Ishigaki no longer has to match a chef's dishes, but he has never eased up on the innovation. Every month he introduces three new cocktails, often classics reworked with fresh fruit or vegetables—a kumquat Alexander, a passion fruit French 75, a white peach G&T, a kiwi-and-pistachio Whiskey Sour—using produce bought directly from farmers. And he makes them with unusual speed. Ishigaki's movements are as seamless as any other top bartender's, but they are much, much faster.

He says speed was never the aim, though: "It's just what happened when I stripped away unnecessary movements. I think it's better to focus on taste, remove what's just for show, and speed up."

— BLOOD RED DIAMOND —

BAR RAGE, AOYAMA

Jameson Irish Whiskey ran a "farm-to-glass" cocktail contest in 2019, and former IT engineer Atsushi Nakamura won it with something that tastes like licking your fingers after a day tilling fields—in a good way. It's earthy and juicy, made with potatoes and beets from his home prefecture of Saitama.

GLASSWARE: Cocktail glass

- 1¹/₅ oz. | 35 ml Jameson Irish Whiskey
- ½ oz. | 15 ml Houjicha Honey Water
- 2 bar spoons Roasted Sweet Potato Juice
- 1 bar spoon fresh beet juice

1. Add all of the ingredients to a mixing glass with ice, stir until chilled, and strain into a cocktail glass.

HOUJICHA HONEY WATER: Combine 1 part honey with 1 part brewed houjicha tea and let it cool before using or storing.

ROASTED SWEET POTATO JUICE: Preheat the oven to 400°F (200°C) and roast 1 sweet potato until the flesh is tender, about 1 hour. Remove from the oven and scrape the sweet potato's flesh into a blender. Add 3 parts water and puree until smooth. Strain through cheesecloth before using or storing.

HOSHIKO

Even before he was known as the creator of Japan's best umeshu, Sei-jiro "Danny" Aikawa was a big influence on a segment of the Tokyo bar scene. He rode a Harley, wore a hoodie behind the bar, and was the rock 'n' roll antithesis of the bow-tied classicists. He named his bar Howl, after the Allen Ginsberg poem, and it drew an audience of bikers, photographers, musicians, and designers. Aikawa thought bar-tending needed an image overhaul, bartenders needed to have more fun, and it had to become a profession young people aspired to join, which at the time, he says, it was not.

But before all that, Aikawa dropped out of college and flew to New York City, where he spent five years doing "nothing but playing around." When he returned to Tokyo in the late '70s he found bar work in the Harajuku scene, serving people who would become world-famous musicians. But as he surveyed his back bar he wondered why all the ingredients came from abroad, and decided he wanted to make a premium liquor that was pure Japanese and captured the country's climate, culture, and terroir. And perhaps a little of his personality: "I like the fact that ume fruit can be poisonous or medicinal depending on how you treat them," he says.

It took him 17 years to perfect the recipe. "You can only make umeshu once a year, when the fruit is in season," he says. "And there are so many variables, so many spirits, different kinds of ume, different sugars, herbs, spices."

Once he had his recipe, he invited trusted bartender friends to test it out. It was his moonshine period, flying under the taxman's radar, until Hoshiko went licit in 2005 with the backing of a major drinks company.

Now, each November 1, the latest batch of Hoshiko is released, and these days it reaches bars in Hong Kong, Australia, Europe, and even Aikawa's old home, New York City.

Aikawa is now in semi-retirement, working occasionally in Higashiyama, a bar run by interior design superstar Shinichiro Ogata. The hoodie has been replaced by a suit, which he describes as "cosplay" to match his new chic home. His menu features eight Hoshiko-based cocktails, but he says there is no reason to feature any of them here. "Recipe books are boring," he says. "Nobody needs them." So, instead, here are three great Hoshiko cocktails from other bartenders.

— THE LAST BASTARD —

BAR TRENCH, EBISU

"We've seen the Suffering Bastard cocktail, the Dying Bastard, the Dead Bastard. To close the saga: The Last Bastard," says Bar Trench's Rogerio Igarashi Vaz, an early promoter of Hoshiko and former customer of Howl.

GLASSWARE: Tiki mug

GARNISH: Dehydrated lemon wheel, mint, dried chili, ground allspice

- ⅔ oz. | 20 ml Fair Gin
- ⅔ oz. | 20 ml Hoshiko Umeshu
- ⅔ oz. | 20 ml Bigallet China-China Amer Liqueur
- ⅔ oz. | 20 ml fresh orange juice
- 2 bar spoons fresh lime juice
- 2 dashes Dale DeGroff's Pimento Aromatic Bitters

1. Add all of the ingredients, except for the bitters, to a tiki mug.

2. Insert a swizzle stick and half fill with crushed ice.

3. Place your palms on either side of the stick and rub back and forth, then move the stick up and down.

4. Top with more crushed ice and then bitters.

SWIZZLE STICKS

The original swizzle sticks were multi-pronged dried twigs from a tree native to the Caribbean. They had spikes at the end like the base of a hat stand. In the early 20th century, boorish British aristocrats used them to whizz the bubbles out of sparkling wine. When tiki cocktails took off in the U.S., the wood gave way to plastic giraffes and palm trees. But skip the gear: swizzling with a bar spoon works perfectly well.

– H&N –

AO, NIHONBASHI

Gin, Campari, and umeshu looks like Negroni territory, but the woody notes from the barrel-aged Kyrö gin and spices from the umeshu make this more like a Boulevardier. Creator Soran Nomura spent the first decade of his career in London, but the immigration people sent him back to Japan.

GLASSWARE: Old Fashioned

GARNISH: Strip of lemon zest

- 1 oz. | 30 ml Kyrö Koskue Barrel-Aged Gin
- 1 oz. | 30 ml Campari
- ⅔ oz. | 20 ml Hoshiko Umeshu
- 1 strip of lemon zest

1. Build the cocktail over ice in an Old Fashioned glass. Add the strip of lemon zest and stir until chilled.

— A NIGHT IN TUNISIA —

BAR QWANG, NISHI AZABU

Yasuhiro Hasegawa's first mentor was a Mori Bar (see page 34) graduate who admired Danny Aikawa and fused their rather contrasting styles. Hasegawa later found himself working alongside Aikawa in a restaurant bar, and was one of the trusted friends who tested Hoshiko before its commercial release. He's found the perfect balance of bitter, sweet, and sour with a cocktail named after the song that happened to be playing the first time a customer asked what the drink was called.

GLASSWARE: Coupe

- 1 oz. | 30 ml Hoshiko Umeshu
- 1 oz. | 30 ml Becherovka
- ½ oz. | 15 ml fresh lemon juice
- 1 egg white
- 1 dash Bob's Liquorice Bitters

1. Add all of the ingredients with ice to a cocktail shaker, shake vigorously, and strain into a coupe.

CONTEMPORARY
COCKTAILS

GASTRONOMY CRYSTAL GAZPACHO *

GASTRONOMY CHOCOLATE MARTINI *

CHOCOLATE BURDOCK MARTINI *

PANDA LATINO * FAKE GIMLET *

DUMMY MILK PUNCH * TAMACHI *

BLUE CHEESE MARTINI * DONS OF SOUL

* YAKUMI PENICILLIN * LAUGH * HERBAL

SICILIANO * SATOYAMA OLD FASHIONED

* APOTHECARY GIMLET * CHERRY

CHERRY MONKEY * OLIVE OIL GIMLET *

LAPSANG SOUCHONG * IRISH BREEZE *

BLACK GIMLET * LONG ISLAND ICED TEA

* GYOKURO & ABSINTHE COCKTAIL *

HOT BLOODY MARY * PERFECT NIKKA *

SPICY BLOODY MARY

"I think all liquids can go into cocktails. I have to try them all."
—SHUZO NAGUMO

The orthodox style of bartending thrived in Japan partly because there was little exposure to what was happening elsewhere. International travel was beyond the means of most bartenders, inbound tourism was negligible, and most of the people making cocktails could speak no English. None of those things are true anymore, and the cocktail culture is changing fast.

— GASTRONOMY CRYSTAL GAZPACHO —

THE SOCIETY, PARK HOTEL TOKYO, SHIODOME

Hotel bar The Society is named for its ties to the Scotch Malt Whisky Society and its extensive collection of their single-cask malts, but its cocktail program is just as impressive. The highlights are Koji Nammoku's creative culinary-themed drinks, including this gazpacho that's every bit as refreshing as the soup.

GLASSWARE: Wine glass

GARNISH: Cucumber slice, rosemary sprig, 3 slices of mini tomato, 2 dashes orange-flavored olive oil

- 1 oz. | 30 ml Tomato Gin
- 2 bar spoons Bread St-Germain
- 2 bar spoons Noilly Prat Dry Vermouth
- ½ oz. | 15 ml Tomato Shrub
- 1⅓ oz. | 40 ml tonic water
- 1 oz. | 30 ml soda water

1. Combine gin, St-Germain, vermouth, and the shrub in a cocktail shaker, shake vigorously, and pour over ice into the wine glass.

2. Add the tonic water and soda water.

3. Add the tomato slices, wrap the cucumber slice around the rosemary and insert into the drink, then add the olive oil.

TOMATO GIN: Blend 6 cherry tomatoes with 250 ml Beefeater 24 Gin, refrigerate for 3 hours, then strain through a coffee filter before bottling or using.

BREAD ST-GERMAIN: Vacuum pack 30 grams of well-baked French bread with 200 ml St-Germain Elderflower Liqueur. Cook in a sous-vide machine for 2 hours at 140°F (60°C). Strain through a coffee filter before bottling or using.

TOMATO SHRUB: Heat 300 grams tomato water and 150 grams sugar in a pot and simmer over low heat for 5 minutes. Add a splash of white balsamic vinegar.

— GASTRONOMY CHOCOLATE MARTINI —

THE SOCIETY, PARK HOTEL TOKYO, SHIODOME

Koji Nammoku thinks more like a patissier than a bartender when he makes this martini, melting chocolate rather than reaching for a chocolate liqueur. He says it's essential to use a room-temperature vodka, because a chilled one will cause the chocolate to set. And he advises a light touch with the yuzu.

GLASSWARE: Double martini

GARNISH: Yuzu peel

- 2 tablespoons Valrhona Chocolate (56% cacao)
- 1 oz. | 30 ml Grey Goose Vodka
- 1 oz. | 30 ml fresh cream
- 1 bar spoon truffle-infused honey*

1. Dissolve the chocolate in a hot water bath.

2. Combine all the ingredients with ice in a Boston shaker, shake well, and pour through a tea strainer into the glass.

3. Express the yuzu peel toward the cocktail and discard.

Nammoku uses a commercially available truffle-infused honey. To create some at home: warm 80 grams of honey in a hot water bath, shave winter truffle into it and stir. Remove from heat, cover, and let rest for at least one day.

— CHOCOLATE BURDOCK MARTINI —

PR BAR, GAIENMAE

Burdock has been used in beverages for at least a millennium. The Europeans added it to gruit, an early bittering agent for beer. Brits ferment it with dandelion stems. Americans have it in root beer. In Japan, it has always been something to eat, not drink, but here its delectable earthiness balances the sweetness of the chocolate and sherry.

GLASSWARE: Coupe

GARNISH: Burdock slice

- 2 oz. | 60 ml Burdock and Cacao Nib Brandy
- ½ oz. | 15 ml Chocolate liqueur
- 2 bar spoons Pedro Ximénez sherry
- 1 bar spoon maple syrup
- 3 dashes orange bitters

1. Combine all ingredients in a cocktail shaker with ice, shake vigorously, and strain into the coupe over an ice block.

2. Garnish with the burdock slice.

BURDOCK AND CACAO NIB BRANDY: Place one stick of raw burdock and 10 grams of cacao nibs in 700 ml of brandy and let rest for 3 days. Strain before using or bottling.

— PANDA LATINO —

ROOFTOP BAR, ANDAZ TOKYO TORANOMON HILLS, TORANOMON

Every season, the bartenders at the Andaz Hotel's 52nd-floor bar each have to devise a new fresh-fruit cocktail. This alcohol-free drink, by Hungarian Lionel Robin Ódor, who spent a year with the bar from summer 2018, is herbal, sour, and ever-so-slightly salty. For a boozy version, add ⅔ oz. (20 ml) of vodka or gin and switch out the syrup for St-Germain Elderflower Liqueur.

GLASSWARE: Double-tall old fashioned
GARNISH: Slice of kiwi and sprigs of rosemary

- 1 kiwi fruit, peeled
- 1⅓ oz. | 40 ml Herb Tea
- ⅔ oz. | 20 ml elderflower syrup
- 2 bar spoons fresh lemon juice
- ⅓ bar spoon freshly grated Parmesan cheese

1. Place all ingredients in a mixing glass and combine with a hand blender.

2. Half fill the glass with crushed ice and pour the cocktail over the ice.

3. Top with more crushed ice and garnish with the kiwi and rosemary.

HERB TEA: Brew rosemary, thyme, oregano, and black pepper. Let it sit overnight, then strain before bottling or using. Ódor says the precise herb ratio isn't important, but the strength of the tea is, because it plays the role of the spirit.

— FAKE GIMLET —

CIELITO LINDO BAR & GRILL, TAKESHIBA

In 2014, Beefeater Gin sent Naoya Ohtake to London for the global final of a cocktail contest and set up a seminar with mixologist Ryan Chetiyawardana. He says it was eye-opening, and when he returned home he began playing with acids and cryoextraction. He makes his Fake Gimlet because, he says, he likes the taste of lime but not the smell, and because it's more sustainable than flying the fruit in.

GLASSWARE: Cocktail glass

- 1½ oz. | 45 ml Blended Gin
- ⅔ oz. | 20 ml Fake Lime Juice
- 1½ bar spoons | 7.5 ml Darjeeling Syrup

1. Place a large ice cube or ball in a cocktail glass.

2. Combine all the ingredients in a cocktail shaker with ice, shake vigorously, and strain into the cocktail glass.

BLENDED GIN: Combine 230 ml Plymouth Gin, 80 ml Tanqueray No. Ten Gin, 30 ml G-Vine Gin, and 20 ml Le Gin in a bottle and store.

FAKE LIME JUICE: Combine 8 grams citric acid, 6 grams malic acid, 0.2 grams tartaric acid, and 0.06 grams succinic acid in 200 ml water. Stir until dry ingredients have dissolved and store.

DARJEELING SYRUP: Add 10 grams loose-leaf darjeeling tea to 150 ml simple syrup and heat in a sous vide at 120°F (50°C) for 45 minutes.

– DUMMY MILK PUNCH –

CIELITO LINDO BAR & GRILL, TAKESHIBA

Most of Naoya Ohtake's recipes are as complicated as the one on the previous page, but this is a rare simple one for a milk punch without the milk.

GLASSWARE: Cocktail glass
GARNISH: Strip of lemon peel

- 1 oz. | 30 ml Beefeater Gin
- ⅔ oz. | 20 ml umeshu
- 2 bar spoons Malibu Rum

1. Add all of the ingredients with ice to a mixing glass, stir, and strain into a cocktail glass. Garnish with the strip of lemon peel.

Ohtake also makes a mocktail version, switching the gin out for the nonalcoholic distillate Seedlip Grove 42, and burning off the alcohol in the umeshu and Malibu.

— TAMACHI —

*S*ingapore-based cocktail consultants Compound Collective devised the first menu for the Pullman Tokyo hotel's rooftop bar and offered this clever, alcohol-free drink that doesn't feel like a compromise at all.

GLASSWARE: Coupe
GARNISH: 3 drops of sesame oil

- 1½ oz. | 45 ml Shiso Cordial
- 1⅓ oz. | 40 ml fresh lemon juice
- ⅔ oz. | 20 ml Butterfly Pea Water

1. Add all of the ingredients to a cocktail shaker with ice, shake vigorously, and strain into a coupe. Garnish with 3 drops of sesame oil.

SHISO CORDIAL: Place 200 ml water, 200 grams sugar, and 25 ml vodka in a saucepan and warm over medium heat, stirring to dissolve the sugar. Using a wand lighter or a long match, flame off any remaining alcohol, remove the pan from heat, and add 20 shiso leaves. Steep for 1 hour. Stir in 1 gram citric acid and strain before using or storing.

BUTTERFLY PEA WATER: Steep 1 cup of loose-leaf butterfly pea tea in 1 liter of hot water for 10 minutes. Strain before using or storing.

SHUZO NAGUMO'S MIXOLOGY BARS

In his college days, Shuzo Nagumo thought he could bluff his way into the famously exacting world of Japanese bartending. At an interview in his native Okayama, a restaurant bar manager asked if he knew how to make cocktails. "Yes," he lied, and got the job, but was rumbled almost immediately.

That setback spurred him to study and practice until he earned his place back behind that bar. He began mixing cocktail history's greatest hits, plus tropical novelties such as Sex on the Beach and French Cactus (a Margarita without the lime juice; bigger in Japan than elsewhere.)

His interest in mixology was piqued by the book *Cool Cocktails* by Ben Reed of London's Met Bar, released in 2000. "I thought the recipes were very interesting: Port wine flips, Strawberry Martinis, basil-and-something cocktails. I thought 'This is the future. I should learn that.'"

From there his path went a little unorthodox. He spent a year as a real estate salesman, then moved to London to work in the kitchen at Nobu, which sat in the same hotel as the Met Bar.

By 2009, Nagumo was back in Japan and ready to open his own space. He called it Code Name Mixology and crafted a menu focused on quirky infusions. "I tried many, many infusions, every day, every night, for two years," he says, but he rates it only a qualified success. People weren't sure what to make of it all.

Instead of folding, he doubled down. He opened a sister bar equipped with a smoke gun, liquid nitrogen, a sous vide, and a rotary evaporator, then flew to London, to the laboratory of pioneering mixologist Tony Conigliaro, to learn how to use it.

Back in Japan, Nagumo began by replicating Conigliaro's recipes. "I made horseradish vodka, ginger vodka . . . delicious," he says. Then he started playing. Blue cheese, wasabi, foie gras, porcini, oysters, Parmesan, sansho, anything with an aroma went into the gizmo with gin, vodka, Cognac, or rum. When he was happy with a distillate, he would develop a cocktail with it. "First I tried using them in classic recipes . . . so terrible," he says. "Then I started thinking in terms of flavor profiles. Foie gras suits things sweet and rich, so I made the Gastro-Chocolate Martini." That's foie gras vodka, homemade Valrhona ganache, double cream, and nutmeg, served inside a bag of smoke.

This time, Nagumo's outside-the-box approach produced a smash hit, and just in time for the Instagram era. A flurry of other bars followed suit, including the speakeasy Mixology Laboratory, the tea-centric Mixology Salon (see page 267), and the shochu-focused Mixology Spirits Bang (see page 283).

Nagumo opened his seventh bar in June 2020, focused on cocktails using cacao, herbs, and rose petals, and in fall 2020 he opened an eighth, Mixology Heritage, that offers "perfected classics."

When Nagumo describes his vision, he sounds like the intelligence boss M from the Bond movies. Each bar has a mission—to popularize botanical cocktails or tea cocktails or shochu or cacao—and each head bartender is an agent assigned to the case. He wants them to build a new category within the drinks world, to push the industry in a new direction, and hopefully one day break off and open their own place. And just like M's operatives, they'll have all the hi-tech gadgets they might need.

— BLUE CHEESE MARTINI —

CODE NAME MIXOLOGY, AKASAKA

It makes perfect sense if you think about it: grapes, honey, and cheese. Shuzo Nagumo says he was making the cocktail with blue cheese vodka in the early days, but switching to Cognac was a revelation.

GLASSWARE: Cocktail glass

GARNISH: Olive

- 1½ oz. | 45 ml Roquefort Cognac
- ½ oz. | 15 ml Sauternes
- 1 bar spoon agave nectar

1. Add all of the ingredients to a tasting glass and stir until combined.

2. Transfer the mixture to a mixing glass with ice, stir until chilled, and strain into a cocktail glass. Garnish with the olive.

ROQUEFORT COGNAC: Melt 350 grams Roquefort cheese in a pan, transfer to a large jar, add 700 ml Hennessy VS Cognac and mix with a hand blender. Transfer to a flask and distill in a rotary evaporator at a pressure of 30 mbar, with the hot bath at 100°F (38°C). Gradually increase the rotation speed from 50 to 150 rpm. When you have extracted 500 ml, add 150 ml mineral water, bottle it, and store at room temperature.

– DONS OF SOUL –

SPIRITS BAR SUNFACE, SHINJUKU

Think Margarita plus salsa. Koji Esashi won Jose Cuervo's international Don of Tequila contest with this drink in 2015. His reward was to blend and bottle his own tequila on the Cuervo estate.

GLASSWARE: Cocktail glass

GARNISH: Strip of lime peel

- 1⅔ oz. | 48 ml Jose Cuervo Especial Silver Tequila
- 1 oz. | 30 g fresh tomato
- ⅔ oz. | 20 g fresh paprika
- 2 bar spoons fresh lime juice
- 2 bar spoons fresh lemon juice
- 1 bar spoon agave nectar
- ¼ teaspoon red chilli powder
- 1 pinch pink pepper
- 1 dash Bob's Coriander Bitters

1. Place all of the ingredients in a container and use a hand blender to combine.

2. Strain the mixture into a cocktail shaker, add ice, and shake vigorously.

3. Strain into a cocktail glass and garnish with the strip of lime peel.

— YAKUMI PENICILLIN —

SPIRITS BAR SUNFACE, SHINJUKU

Yakumi translates as "condiments," and Koji Esashi balances four of them in a spicy, liberal interpretation of the Penicillin.

GLASSWARE: Old Fashioned glass
GARNISH: Myouga leaf

- 1½ oz. | 45 ml mezcal
- ½ oz. | 15 ml fresh lemon juice
- 1 bar spoon honey
- 1 slice fresh ginger
- ½ myouga bud
- 1 pinch fresh wasabi

1. Place all of the ingredients in a container and use a hand blender to combine.

2. Strain the mixture into a cocktail shaker, add ice, and shake vigorously.

3. Strain into an Old Fashioned glass and garnish with the myouga leaf.

— LAUGH —

BAR CAPRI, HOTEL NEW OTANI TOKYO, AKASAKA

The Hotel New Otani Tokyo is a storied place, occupying what was once a feudal lord's estate. It appeared in the Bond movie *You Only Live Twice* as the headquarters of Osato Chemicals, and has hosted prime ministers, presidents, royals, and autocrats. The main bar has a menu with original cocktails spanning six decades, including gems like this from current bar captain Hiroki Yoshida that would make his predecessors' heads spin. Yoshida says he found apple and lactic notes in Johnnie Walker Gold Label and amplified them with a bespoke juice and amazake, Japan's low-alcohol fermented rice drink.

GLASSWARE: Cocktail glass
GARNISH: Cinnamon-dusted dried rosebud

- 1⅓ oz. | 40 ml Johnnie Walker Gold Label Reserve Scotch Whisky
- ⅔ oz. | 20 ml Amazake Falernum
- ½ oz. | 15 ml Apple Pie Juice
- 1 bar spoon fresh lemon juice
- 1 bar spoon loose-leaf ruby orange tea
- Dash of Bob's Orange & Mandarin Bitters

1. Add all of the ingredients to a cocktail shaker with ice, shake vigorously, and strain into a cocktail glass. Garnish with the cinnamon-dusted dried rosebud.

AMAZAKE FALERNUM: Place 250 grams amazake, 250 grams sugar, 1 cinnamon stick, ¼ vanilla bean, ½ teaspoon cardamom pods, ¼ teaspoon whole cloves, 2 slices of lemon, and 2 slices of lime in a saucepan and bring to a simmer over medium heat, stirring to dissolve the sugar. Remove from heat, let cool completely, and strain before using or storing.

APPLE PIE JUICE: Place 300 ml apple juice, ¼ teaspoon cinnamon, and ½ vanilla bean in a saucepan and bring to a boil over medium-high heat. Cook until the mixture has reduced by half and remove from heat. Let cool completely and strain before using or storing.

— HERBAL SICILIANO —

COCKTAIL GASTRONOMY KYU YASUI TOKYO, NISHI AZABU

Former hotel bartender Kyu Yasui veers toward original creations, often featuring fresh fruit. In winter, when kumquats are in season, he'll make this cocktail inspired by pasta sauce: creamy and citrusy, with olive oil as an emulsifier.

GLASSWARE: Coupe

GARNISH: 2 slices of kumquat, 1 slice of ginger, and cardamom seed

- 2 fresh kumquats
- 1⅔ oz. | 50 ml Suntory Roku Gin
- 1 bar spoon extra virgin olive oil
- 2 bar spoons fresh lemon juice
- 1 bar spoon simple syrup
- 1 egg white
- 1 slice of ginger

1. Place the kumquats in a saucepan and muddle. Add the gin and warm the mixture until it is simmering and aromatic. Stir in the olive oil and let the mixture cool.

2. Strain into a cocktail shaker. Add the remaining ingredients with ice, shake vigorously, and strain into a coupe. Garnish with the slices of kumquat, ginger, and cardamom seed.

BEES BAR

Only one bar in Tokyo has professional foragers on the payroll. Bees Bar receives deliveries each week from the forests of Ishikawa. The boxes contain items that have almost certainly never featured in a cocktail anywhere else: Japanese silverberries, Japanese spicebush, koshi-abura leaves, the seeds of the chaste tree, and all manner of forest bounty.

The bartenders steep them or turn them into syrups, then work with bar owner Yoshiro Narisawa to create the cocktails. Narisawa is best known as the chef behind the creative fine-dining restaurant that bears his name. After training in the kitchens of Paul Bocuse, Joel Robuchon, and Frédy Girardet, among others, he returned home to create a culinary style he calls "innovative satoyama cuisine." Satoyama are the small, self-sustaining villages that sit where mountains and farmland meet. It's his spin on sustainable living, referencing the way people used to eat when they would forage, fish, and live off the land.

Narisawa opened Bees Bar in 2018, two blocks from his restaurant, partly to give his guests somewhere to drink after their meal, and partly to promote the satoyama concept beyond the $350-dinner crowd.

He was already employing the foragers to collect berries, bark, leaves, nuts, and twigs for his restaurant. He uses Japanese silverberries in a sauce for game and wraps wagyu in 20-inch shell ginger leaves. In the bar, they muddle the berries with lime for a Cosmopolitan, and grind the leaves to accent a Gimlet.

Each week, the restaurant receives 30 to 50 different woodland items. But even if the flora is exotic, the principles of crafting a cocktail don't change. They're playing with the same flavor camps, balancing sweetness and acidity. They're just doing it with different ingredients.

— SATOYAMA OLD FASHIONED —

BEES BAR, GAIENMAE

The taste of the forest, quite literally. Yoshiro Narisawa adds a complex woody tone to the whisky by infusing a fistful of wood shavings; the infusion hits its peak around the 2-week mark.

GLASSWARE: Old Fashioned glass
GARNISH: 1 slice of yuzu, 1 sprig of fresh kinome, twigs

- 2 bar spoons brown sugar
- Club soda, as needed
- 3 drops vanilla bitters

- 1½ oz. | 45 ml Satoyama Hibiki

1. Place the brown sugar in an Old Fashioned glass and moisten it with club soda.

2. Add the bitters and ice. Add the whisky and stir until chilled.

SATOYAMA HIBIKI: Add lindela, oak, and cedar shavings, twigs from a cinnamon tree, and sansho pepper to 1 (750 ml) bottle of Suntory Hibiki Whisky. Steep for about 2 weeks. Strain before using or storing.

— APOTHECARY GIMLET —

BEES BAR, GAIENMAE

Why would you use lime when you have sudachi, a tart green Japanese citrus fruit? And if you ever find shell ginger leaf, it adds a wonderful green note that elevates a Gimlet.

GLASSWARE: Cocktail glass

GARNISH: Sudachi wheel and shell ginger leaf

- 20 juniper berries
- ¼ shell ginger leaf
- 2 oz. | 60 ml Okuhida Vodka
- ⅔ oz. | 20 ml fresh sudachi juice
- 2 bar spoons simple syrup

1. Use a mortar and pestle to grind the berries and leaf.

2. Add the mixture to a Boston shaker. Add the remaining ingredients and ice, shake vigorously, and strain into a cocktail glass.

3. Garnish with the sudachi wheel and shell ginger leaf.

– CHERRY CHERRY MONKEY –

ROOFTOP BAR, ANDAZ TOKYO TORANOMON HILLS, TORANOMON

"I don't think fruit cocktails have to be sweet or tiki," says Lionel Robin Ódor, who came up with this woody, full-bodied cherry cocktail. He cribbed the pistachio syrup recipe from a former colleague in Hungary. "He used it in a rum and coffee drink, but it's so good you can use it in anything," says Ódor. If you have a smoke gun, you can achieve the effect seen in the photo by sending mizunara smoke into the glass and placing a lid on top of the drink.

GLASSWARE: Brandy snifter
GARNISH: Shiso leaf and edible flowers

- 1½ oz. | 45 ml Monkey Shoulder Blended Scotch Whisky
- 1 oz. | 30 ml Salted Pistachio Syrup
- ½ oz. | 15 ml fresh lime juice
- 8 to 10 cherries
- 5 drops shiso bitters or 1 bar spoon Dover Shiso Liqueur

1. Place all of the ingredients in a container and use a hand blender to combine.

2. Strain the mixture into a cocktail shaker, add ice, and shake vigorously.

3. Strain over an ice cube in a brandy snifter and garnish with the shiso leaf and edible flowers.

SALTED PISTACHIO SYRUP: Place 200 grams raw pistachio nuts in a dry skillet and toast over medium heat until they turn brown. Add the toasted nuts, 1 kilogram sugar, 750 ml warm water, and 1 tablespoon sea salt to a blender and puree until combined. Strain before using or storing in the refrigerator.

− OLIVE OIL GIMLET −

BAR AMBER, NISHI AZABU

B ar Amber has already produced two of Tokyo's mixology stars in Hiroyasu Kayama, who is now at Ben Fiddich (see page 254), and Yuya Nagamine, now mixing drinks in the basement of The SG Club (see page 289). This recipe is from Nagamine, who calls it an Olive Oil Gimlet. It tastes more like a fennel Gimlet.

GLASSWARE: Goblet

- **1½ oz. | 45 ml Tanqueray No. Ten**
- **2 bar spoons Fennel Syrup**
- **2 bar spoons fresh lime juice**
- **3 drops orange-flavored olive oil**
- **1 bar spoon lime zest**

1. Place all of the ingredients in a container and use a hand blender to combine.

2. Add the mixture to a cocktail shaker, add ice, and shake vigorously.

3. Strain into a goblet.

FENNEL SYRUP: Place 100 ml simple syrup and 10 grams fennel seeds in a blender and pulse to combine. Strain before using or storing.

— LAPSANG SOUCHONG —

THE STANDARD, HARAJUKU

"I got tired of being a sommelier, a middleman between the creator and the customer," says Yushi Ando, who once poured wines at Joel Robuchon's restaurant in Tokyo. Ando wanted to create flavors, so in 2018 he opened The Standard. His menu has a section for drinks made using a coffee siphon, including this smoky, resinous tea cocktail.

GLASSWARE: Hot Toddy glass

- 60 ml gin
- 11 ml Calvados
- 15 ml simple syrup
- 180 ml water
- 13 g applewood chips
- 11 g almonds
- 8 g organic loose-leaf lapsang souchong
- 1 lemon peel
- 1 orange peel
- 1 slice of apple
- 1 pinch fresh rosemary

1. Place all of the liquids into the bowl of a coffee siphon. Place the remaining ingredients in the upper chamber and gently brew for 2 minutes. Pour into a Hot Toddy glass.

Note: Only metric measurements are used in this recipe to honor its precision.

— IRISH BREEZE —

UNLIMITED COFFEE BAR, NARIHIRA

At the foot of the Tokyo Sky Tree, Unlimited Coffee is a specialty coffee shop, barista training center, and cocktail bar in one. They shine brightest when they use coffee from their nearby roastery to make creative cocktails—such as this fruity, chilled take on an Irish coffee by co-owner Rena Hirai.

GLASSWARE: Cocktail glass

GARNISH: Strawberry powder and granules of dried raspberry

- ¾ oz. | 25 ml Teeling Irish Whiskey
- 1½ oz. | 45 ml espresso made from Ethiopian beans
- ⅔ oz. | 20 ml Hibiscus Syrup
- 1½ oz. | 45 ml cream, lightly whipped

1. Place the whiskey, espresso and syrup in a mixing glass with ice and stir until chilled.

2. Pour into a cocktail glass and float the whipped cream on top. Garnish with strawberry powder and granules of dried raspberry.

HIBISCUS SYRUP: Place 2 grams of hibiscus tea leaves in 100 grams of simple syrup and rest for 10 days. Strain and store.

— BLACK GIMLET —

UNLIMITED COFFEE BAR, NARIHIRA

The Gesha coffee varietal has a bright fruity acidity, at least in the hands of Unlimited Coffee Roasters. They use it, with the zesty Xoriguer Gin and a citrus infusion, to make a drink that tastes improbably like a Gimlet—without any lime juice.

GLASSWARE: Cocktail glass
GARNISH: Strip of lime peel

- 1½ oz. | 45 ml espresso brewed from Gesha beans
- ⅔ oz. | 20 ml Infused Xoriguer Gin
- ⅔ oz. | 20 ml simple syrup

1. Add all of the ingredients to a cocktail shaker with ice, shake vigorously, and strain into a cocktail glass. Garnish with the strip of lime peel.

INFUSED XORIGUER GIN: Add 0.5 grams juniper berries, 0.3 grams jasmine tea, 0.3 grams lemon peel, 0.3 grams lime peel, and 0.3 grams apple mint to 45 ml Xoriguer Gin and steep for 24 hours. Strain before using or storing.

— LONG ISLAND ICED TEA —

THE SG CLUB, SHIBUYA

The booziest cocktail ever devised—minus the booze. This is the simple version. At The SG Club, they use a house-made clarified cola syrup, but a colored, commercial version is perfectly adequate.

GLASSWARE: Highball glass

GARNISH: Lemon slice

- 4.5 ml Non-Alcohol Gin
- 27 ml cola syrup
- 4.5 ml agave syrup
- 9 ml cane syrup
- 0.1 g citric acid
- 60 ml soda water

1. Blend all ingredients, except the soda, and pour over ice into the glass.

2. Top with soda water and garnish with a slice of lemon.

NON-ALCOHOL GIN: Distill 750 ml water with 20 grams juniper berries, 10 grams whole coriander seeds, 10 grams orange peel, 10 grams grapefruit peel, 10 grams lemon peel, and 5 grams cardamom.

Note: Only metric measurements are used in this recipe to honor its precision.

BEN FIDDICH

Hiroyasu Kayama grew up on a dairy farm in the town of Chichibu, just north of Tokyo. The cows are gone now, but the farm is churning out something much more interesting: artisanal absinthe. Kayama's childhood bedroom has become a drying room, festooned with branches of wormwood. Outside, propped up on bricks, is his 20-liter alembic.

The absinthe he produces is classic in character, which raises the question: Why bother? Kayama says he wanted to show off the herbs that grow around his parents' farm, but there's more to it than that. This classically trained bartender, who began his career in an orthodox hotel bar, is driven to experiment and innovate. He makes imitations of Suze, Chartreuse, and Campari, and purchased a beehive to produce his own honey. At the time of writing, he had a bottle of Ledaig Whisky strapped to a pillar on the farm. He was keeping an identical bottle indoors to see what effect the elements might have on the aging process. He has tried similar experiments with Ardbeg in a seabed and in a swamp.

At his bar Ben Fiddich, the shelves are loaded with jars of herbs, spices, unconventional infusions, and vintage spirits and liqueurs, some of them centuries old. Kayama stands behind a slice of rugged walnut and asks his guests for a flavor camp or favorite spirit. What happens next is anyone's guess. He might reach for a mortar and pestle and begin grinding spices to spruce up some whisky, he might warm an iron poker over a flame, or scoop something from his 10-liter fermentation tub. He might also make you a straight-up classic, because despite the flourishes and innovations that have made Ben Fiddich a required stop on the Tokyo drinking tour, Kayama will always be a classically trained bartender.

On the back wall of the bar hangs a copy of Sir Edwin Landseer's painting "The Illicit Highland Whisky Still", depicting a huntsman buying some bootleg Scotch: an apt reference for a bar that serves spirits the taxman probably shouldn't hear about. Kayama says his ultimate ambition is to go legitimate and open an absinthe distillery. Don't bet against it.

— GYOKURO & ABSINTHE COCKTAIL —

BEN FIDDICH, SHINJUKU

Hiroyasu Kayama has an impressive range of hot cocktails, including this marriage of his homemade absinthe with rich, shade-grown gyokuro tea.

GLASSWARE: Ceramic tea bowl

GARNISH: Salted cherry blossom

- 2 bar spoons loose-leaf gyokuro tea
- 2 oz. | 60 ml hot water
- 1 oz. | 30 ml absinthe

1. Place the tea in a teapot and add hot water and absinthe. Steep for 2 minutes.

2. Pour into the tea bowl over 1 ice cube.

— HOT BLOODY MARY —

BEN FIDDICH, SHINJUKU

When you plunge a red-hot poker into the glass, the temperature of the drink jumps immediately, some of the liquid evaporates and you end up with a toasted flavor.

GLASSWARE: Hot Toddy glass

- 1 oz. | 30 ml vodka
- 2 oz. | 60 ml tomato juice
- ⅔ oz. | 20 ml apple juice
- 2 drops balsamic vinegar
- ½ teaspoon butter
- 1 bar spoon honey

1. Add the ingredients to a heat-proof glass and stir to combine. Heat a poker to almost 1,000°F (538°C) and plunge it into the drink for 30 seconds.

— PERFECT NIKKA —

BEN FIDDICH, SHINJUKU

I f you don't wish to distill coffee for the splash included in this recipe, substitute regular coffee.

GLASSWARE: Tin bowl

- 1⅔ oz. | 50 ml Nikka Coffey Grain Whisky
- 1 bar spoon Lillet Blanc
- 1 bar spoon Tempus Fugit Crème de Cacao
- 1 bar spoon distilled coffee

1. Add all of the ingredients to a mixing glass with ice, stir, and strain into a tin bowl.

— SPICY BLOODY MARY —

BAR B&F, SHINJUKU

Bar B&F is a fruit brandy specialist, with more than 100 styles of eau de vie. It's also a sister bar of Ben Fiddich, so the cocktails are suitably radical. Hiromi Takanashi incorporates fungi, honey, and the Japanese condiment ponzu into this hot, textured Mary.

GLASSWARE: Goblet

- ⅔ oz. | 20 ml Opihr Gin
- ⅓ oz. |10 ml Boletus Vodka
- 1 tomato
- ⅓ oz. |10 ml fresh lime juice
- 1¼ teaspoons | 7 ml ponzu
- 1 dash celery or umami bitters
- 1 dash Tabasco
- 1 bar spoon honey
- 1 pinch black pepper, plus more to taste
- 1 pinch carrageenan
- 1 pinch truffle salt

1. Place all of the ingredients in a container and use a hand blender to combine.

2. Add the mixture to a Boston shaker, add ice, and shake vigorously.

3. Strain into a goblet, sprinkle additional pepper on top.

BOLETUS VODKA: Wipe 10 grams dried boletus with a damp towel to remove any dirt. Place the boletus and 350 ml Tito's Vodka in a container and refrigerate for 4 days. Strain before using or storing.

GEN YAMAMOTO, AZABU JUBAN

Thanks, but no thanks, said Gen Yamamoto of the chance to appear in this book. "There are strong stereotypes around the word 'cocktail,'" he said. "And I'm not interested in that."

It's a fair concern. When he opened his bar in 2013 he ignored almost every trope of cocktail culture. No shakers, no mixing glasses, no famous recipes. No big pours, no cocktail glasses, no choosing your own drinks.

All of which is why he had to be in this book, and, eventually, he acquiesced. But you won't find a Gen Yamamoto recipe here—his drinks only make sense in his bar, with his service.

Yamamoto began developing his style while making drinks at a Japanese fine-dining restaurant in New York City. In the early days he would pair fresh fruits with a bold spirit, but over time he began to play with shochu, sake, smaller pours, and less aggressive chilling.

When he had fine-tuned his concept, he realized it would only truly work back home in Japan, where unhurried service will win you plaudits, not cost you tips. He found a space in the upmarket Azabu Juban district of Tokyo, furnished it with the pared-back simplicity of a Japanese tea room, and used a 500-year-old slab of Japanese oak as the counter.

Yamamoto uses native herbs, spices, fruits, and vegetables, and frequently finds unexpected matches. Mountain grapes and wasabi suit sparkling sake. Figs go with gin. The drinks are built, not shaken or stirred, and served as a procession of small amusements, like the dishes on a chef's tasting menu.

By some yardsticks, Gen Yamamoto is the city's most Japanese cocktail bar. By others it's the least. Either way, it's one of the must-see bars. Just don't use the C-word.

TEA COCKTAILS

SENCHA GIN TONIC ✦

ROASTED RUM MANHATTAN ✦

JAPANESE NEGRONI ✦

MONSIEUR L'OSIER ✦ MADAME L'OSIER

✦ BROWN & BLACK HIGHBALL ✦

MISTER NINE

Senior Japanese bartenders usually have a matcha recipe up their sleeves. The powdered, shade-grown leaf signifies opulence and has been used in cocktails, in natural form or liqueur, since at least the 1970s. More recently, younger bartenders have begun delving deeper into the country's tea culture, learning to use sun-grown sencha and pot-roasted houjicha in particular.

The ultimate destination for tea cocktails is the eight-seat Mixology Salon, which sits in the middle of a Venn diagram of orthodox bartending, mixology, and tea culture. They serve classics with a tea twist for the traditionalists, experimental creations for the mixology fans, and tea with a bite for those who want the brew, not the spirit, to dominate. Owner Shuzo Nagumo toured the top tea regions—Shizuoka, Fukuoka, and Uji—making connections with the growers and studying the finer points of the production before opening the bar in 2017.

— SENCHA GIN TONIC —

MIXOLOGY SALON, GINZA

The Sencha Gin Tonic has become a modern Japanese classic, but no one makes them better than the bartenders at Mixology Salon. Owner Shuzo Nagumo says it's important to use *fukamushi* ("deep-steamed") tea, which is sweeter, deeper, and smoother than ordinary sencha. And skip the citrus garnish: it clashes with the tea.

GLASSWARE: Tumbler

- **1 oz. | 30 ml Sencha Gin**
- **2.8 oz. | 80 ml Fever Tree Tonic Water**
- **Club soda, as needed**

1. Place three rounded-off ice cubes in a tumbler. Rinse the cubes with club soda and strain.

2. Pour the gin evenly around the glass and between the cubes. Add the tonic, making sure to pour onto the gin, not the ice, and gently stir.

SENCHA GIN: Place 1 tablespoon loose-leaf sencha tea in 1 (750 ml) bottle of gin and steep for 1 day. Strain before using or storing in the refrigerator. Nagumo recommends Bombay Sapphire, Tanqueray, or Roku, and says to avoid gins with dominant citrus notes.

— ROASTED RUM MANHATTAN —

Two long-aged spirits, two vermouths, and some roasted green tea make for an after-dinner sipper with a long and layered palate.

GLASSWARE: Cocktail glass

GARNISH: Griottine or black cherry

- 1½ oz. | 45 ml Houjicha Rum
- 1 bar spoon Daniel Bouju XO Cognac

- ½ oz. | 15 ml Carpano Antico Formula sweet vermouth
- 1 bar spoon Carpano Punto e Mes vermouth

1. Add ingredients to a tasting glass and stir without ice. Add the mixture to a mixing glass, add ice, and stir once.

2. Strain into a cocktail glass and garnish with a griottine or black cherry.

HOUJICHA RUM: Place 1 tablespoon loose-leaf houjicha tea in 1 (750 ml) bottle of Ron Zacapa Centenario 23 Rum and let steep overnight. Strain before using or storing.

— JAPANESE NEGRONI —

BAR LEGACY, SHIBUYA

The combination of Campari, Martini Bitter, and houjicha creates a softer, more natural bitterness than you get with Campari alone.

GLASSWARE: Old Fashioned glass
GARNISH: Houjicha leaves

- ⅔ oz. | 20 ml Houjicha Vodka
- ⅔ oz. | 20 ml Mancino Rosso Vermouth
- 2 bar spoons Campari, chilled
- 2 bar spoons Martini & Rossi Bitter, chilled

1. Build the cocktail in an Old Fashioned glass containing an ice ball and stir, slowly, putting air in the drink without melting the ice.

2. Sprinkle houjicha onto the top of the ice ball. Use enough to give a nose, but not so much that it slides into the drink.

HOUJICHA VODKA: Add 15 grams of loose-leaf houjicha tea to 1 (750 ml) bottle of vodka and steep for 2 days. Strain before using or storing.

BAR LEGACY

By the time Atsushi Yoshikawa opened Bar Legacy in
2015 he had served an 18-
year apprenticeship under
two of the city's bartending
greats—the late Kenji Otsuki
of Ginza's Bar OPA, and Shinobu Ishigaki of Ishinohana
(see page 196)—and won
himself a national trophy for
cocktail technique. Rarely
has anyone been more ready.
He now works behind an
800-year-old slice of bubinga
one block from Shibuya
Station. There he combines
the orthodoxy of his Ginza
beginnings with the user-
friendliness of his Shibuya
years. His classics have been
given two decades of
thought, he has original recipes for those who seek innovation, and his fruit-and-veg
cocktail menu often features
citrus fruits even locals
barely know.

— MONSIEUR L'OSIER —

BAR CAESAREAN, YOYOGI UEHARA

The vivid green color is a throwback, but the taste is timeless. This was created by Kazuo Uyeda (see page 39) when he ran Shiseido's Bar L'Osier. It was introduced to me at Bar Caesarean, where Toshiaki Tanaka still follows the recipe he learned from his mentor 30 years ago.

GLASSWARE: Cocktail glass

- 1⅓ oz. | 40 ml gin
- 2 bar spoons green tea liqueur
- 2 bar spoons fresh lime juice

1. Add all of the ingredients to a cocktail shaker with ice, shake vigorously, and strain into a cocktail glass.

— MADAME L'OSIER —

BAR CAESAREAN, YOYOGI UEHARA

The dessert counterpart to the Monsieur L'Osier (see previous page) is opulent and indulgent.

GLASSWARE: Coupe

- 1⅓ oz. | 40 ml Cognac
- 2 bar spoons green tea liqueur
- 2 bar spoons cream

1. Add all of the ingredients to a cocktail shaker with ice, shake vigorously, and strain into a coupe.

— BROWN & BLACK HIGHBALL —

BAR AVANTI, GINZA

Kana Arai makes a cold-brew houjicha and runs it through a soda siphon to make a highball that pairs superbly with the curries her bar is famous for. She says she chose the tea to suit the smoky notes in the Scotch.

GLASSWARE: Highball glass

- 1⅔ oz. | 50 ml Johnnie Walker Black Scotch Whisky
- 1 brown sugar cube
- ½ teaspoon | 3 ml Houjicha Bitters
- 3⅓ oz. | 100 ml houjicha soda

1. Add the whisky, sugar cube, and bitters to a chilled highball glass and muddle.

2. Add ice and top with the houjicha soda.

HOUJICHA BITTERS: In a bowl, combine 7 grams loose-leaf houjicha (pan-roasted green tea) and 90 ml Johnnie Walker Black Label Whisky and let rest for 2 hours. Strain through a coffee filter and store.

— MISTER NINE —

SUZU BAR, SHINJUKU

In the post-war years, the Golden Gai district was a warren of brothels and black market shops, but the prostitutes left long ago and bartenders moved in. For cocktail fans, the pick of the bunch is Suzu Bar, opened in 2014 by a family that runs the tonkatsu restaurant Suzuya in a nearby red-light district. The signature bar snack is, naturally, a tonkatsu sandwich.

GLASSWARE: Old Fashioned glass
GARNISH: Bay leaf

- 1 oz. | 30 ml Jasmine-Infused Gin
- ½ oz. | 15 ml bourbon
- ½ oz. | 15 ml St-Germain

1. Build the cocktail in an Old Fashioned glass containing one large cube of ice and garnish with a bay leaf.

JASMINE-INFUSED GIN: Combine 1 teaspoon loose-leaf jasmine tea with 700 ml of gin and steep for 1 minute. Strain before using or storing.

SHOCHU COCKTAILS

"In the beginning, I was just thinking it's embarrassing we don't make cocktails with our national spirit," says Shuzo Nagumo of the Mixology bar group. "Then I started studying it, and the more you learn, the more interesting it gets."

He's talking about shochu, the distillate that dates back to medieval times. It is Japan's most popular spirit, outselling all others combined. In 2018, Japanese people drank more than 750 million liters of it in izakayas, in karaoke boxes, in yakitori joints, and at home—but they drank almost none in cocktail bars.

Shochu has traditionally been shunned by the cocktail community for several reasons. Most is bottled at 25% abv, which is an awkward fit for standard ratios. Prestige shochu, called honkaku, is distilled just once in a pot still, and can taste a little funky and brash. And perhaps most importantly, shochu is not an aspirational drink for Tokyo's citizens. It does not transport them mentally to Speyside, Kentucky, or the Charente. It conjures up cheap drinks after work. Fun, yes; fancy, no.

Nagumo wanted to change that, so in late 2018 he opened Mixology Spirits Bang in Ginza. Officially it's devoted to all Japanese alcohol. While it has an impressive range of domestic gins and whiskies, shochu cocktails dominate, from elevated versions of izakaya standards to avant-garde works like the one that employs roasted potato skins to fashion a drink that loosely resembles a vintage Port.

"I know it's a bit early for this kind of bar," says Nagumo. "But I believe shochu is going to be a global spirit. Change is coming."

Shingo Gokan thinks so too. The founder of The SG Club teamed up with three distillers to release a collection of shochus.

Leading the project was Joshin Atone, a bartender who has worked for Gokan in New York, Shanghai, and now Tokyo, and whose family hails from the shochu heartland of Kyushu.

Atone says the inspiration for the SG bottles was the realization that bartenders are using mezcal from tiny estates in Mexico and piscos from farms in Peru but ignoring the spirit closest to his heart. "People don't even consider it in their repertoire," he says. "Even if you're a famous bartender who's studied spirits in depth, shochu won't usually make it onto the list."

The SG team created three expressions: one made from barley, one from rice, and one from sweet potato. Shochu is distilled from a mash of saccharized rice or barley that has been fermented with one defining ingredient. Barley, rice, and sweet potato are the category leaders.

Atone spent a week at each distillery, working on the recipes and learning the nuances of the production. "There's a lot you can control," he says. "The ingredients, the type of koji (a saccharizing fungus), the yeast, the distillation and aging process . . . you can tune each of those aspects to get the desired character. Filtering at the end, for example, removing some of the oils, makes it work a lot better with cocktails and fruit."

They bottled all three styles at a bar-friendly 38 to 40 percent ABV, and both Gokan and Atone see the pungency as a merit, not a problem, for the modern bartender. "Single distilled is always better," says Gokan, "because you get more of the original ingredient." "When your base spirit has a lot of inherent flavors it actually allows for a lot of creativity from the bartender," says Atone.

The creativity is on display at his bar now, where shochu is as prominent as whisky or gin on the menu. "We'd like the world to know: Hey, there's this thing we've been doing for quite a long time and it's actually quite refined," says Atone.

TUMUGI

The people who make The SG Club's barley shochu didn't need any convincing to target the cocktail market. Sanwa Shurui, Japan's second-biggest shochu maker, was already there: just not with shochu exactly.

The company makes Tumugi (say: Tsu-moo-gee), a spirit based on koji, the fungus that's essential in the production of miso, mirin, soy sauce, sake . . . and shochu.

At their distillery on the island of Kyushu, Sanwa Shurui creates the phenomenally popular Iichiko shochu by fermenting a mash of barley and koji, then adding much more steamed barley, fermenting again, and sending the mash through a pot still.

To make Tumugi, they infuse the mash with mint, lemon, mandarin, yuzu, and kabosu, distill in a continuous still, then blend the result with a pot-still shochu that has a bold koji character, and bottle it at 80 proof.

They released it in 2015 and though it isn't proving any threat to shochu as Japan's signature spirit, it has gained an avid following among bartenders both orthodox and experimental. (See pages 293-295 for Tumugi recipes.)

— EMULS —

Some shochu producers bottle the "heads" of their distillation, the first part that distillers usually discard. Called *hanatare,* it is potent and intense. Shuzo Nagumo uses a brown-sugar hanatare called Fau, smooths off the edges with a brown-butter wash, then pairs it with some sub-tropical friends.

GLASSWARE: Champagne flute

GARNISH: Finely grated coconut

- 1⅓ oz. | 40 ml Brown Butter–Washed Hanatare Shochu
- ½ oz. | 15 ml fresh lemon juice
- ⅛ pineapple
- 1 bar spoon orgeat syrup
- ½ teaspoon | 3 ml white sesame oil

1. Add all ingredients to a shaker and emulsify with a hand mixer.

2. Double-strain into a champagne flute.

BROWN BUTTER–WASHED HANATARE: Place 150 grams butter in a pan and melt over medium heat. When it begins to bubble, remove from heat and add 1 (750 ml) bottle of brown-sugar hanatare shochu. Stir gently and let sit for 2 hours at room temperature. Strain through a coffee filter before using or storing in the refrigerator.

— THE JAPANESE COCKTAIL —

THE SG CLUB, SHIBUYA

This cocktail reverses the custom of serving green tea with wagashi confectionary, putting the wagashi flavors in the drink and the green tea on the side.

GLASSWARE: Coupe

GARNISH: Matcha-dusted warabi mochi

- 1½ oz. | 45 ml Japanese Mix
- ½ oz. | 15 ml Mugwort Shochu
- ½ oz. | 15 ml water
- 1 bar spoon wasanbon sugar
- Spritz of salt water

1. Add all of the ingredients, except for the salt water, to a mixing glass with ice, stir, and strain into a coupe.

2. Spritz with the salt water and garnish with the matcha-dusted warabi mochi.

JAPANESE MIX: Heat 500 ml soy milk and 3 grams agar agar and allow to dissolve. Add another 500 ml soy milk, 1 liter SG Kome shochu, 100 grams *kinako* (roasted soy flour), and 400 grams molasses. Mix well, remove from heat and refrigerate for 6 to 12 hours. Strain through a cheesecloth before using or storing.

MUGWORT SHOCHU: Combine 10 grams dry mugwort and 1 (750 ml) bottle of SG Kome Shochu and steep for 24 hours at room temperature. Strain before using or storing.

— POTATO STOCKING —

TIGRATO, YOTSUYA

This clever riff on the Silk Stocking calls for sweet potato shochu where the tequila usually goes, and amazake in place of the cream. Creator Katsuyoshi Chikazawa says the Moriizou brand of shochu works best, but any quality potato shochu will do.

GLASSWARE: Coupe

- 1 oz. | 30 ml sweet potato shochu
- ¾ oz. | 28 ml white crème de cacao
- ⅓ oz. | 10 ml amazake
- 1 dash Luxardo

1. Add all of the ingredients to a cocktail shaker with ice, shake vigorously, and double-strain into a coupe.

— TUMUGI COCKTAIL —

BAR ROCAILLE, SHIBUYA

The koji of the Tumugi and the lactic notes of the yogurt combine to create an aroma like the air of a sake brewery.

GLASSWARE: Highball glass

GARNISH: Strip of orange peel

- ⅔ oz. | 20 ml Tumugi
- ½ oz. | 15 ml yogurt liqueur
- Sweet ginger ale, to top

1. Add 2 large ice cubes to a highball glass.

2. Add the Tumugi, then the liqueur, and top with ginger ale. Lift with a spoon to combine.

— TUMUGIM —

HIBIYA BAR WAPIRITS, GINZA

At Hibiya Bar Wapirits you can have any spirit you want—so long as it's Tumugi. Bamboos, Negronis, Grasshoppers, Piña Coladas, White Ladies and a host of other classics get a Tumugi makeover, but the menu highlight is this house original that uses the Japanese condiment mirin for depth.

GLASSWARE: Cocktail glass

- 1½ oz. | 45 ml Tumugi
- ½ oz. | 15 ml fresh lime juice
- ½ bar spoon dark mirin
- ½ bar spoon simple syrup

1. Add all of the ingredients to a cocktail shaker with ice, shake vigorously, and strain into a cocktail glass.

— TENTATION —

BAR AVANTI, GINZA

The Ginza district's greatest Tumugi fan is the Takao Mori-mentored Yuu Okazaki of the all-female Bar Avanti. Her signature cocktail is a complex, tropical masterpiece.

GLASSWARE: Cocktail glass

GARNISH: Peppercorns

- ¾ oz. | 25 ml Tumugi
- ½ oz. | 15 ml lychee liqueur
- 2 bar spoons peach liqueur
- 2 bar spoons mango puree
- 1 bar spoon Monin Elderflower Syrup
- 2 bar spoons fresh lemon juice
- ⅓ bar spoon ginger juice
- 1 pinch ground cardamom
- 2 dashes Abbot's Bitters

1. Add all of the ingredients to a cocktail shaker with ice, shake vigorously, and double-strain into a cocktail glass. Garnish with peppercorns.

SAKE COCKTAILS

L. I. T. ✦ TAIKOH ✦ SHUNGYO ✦

THE TIME ✦ TRENCH 75 ✦ AJISAI ✦

OOZAKURA

The 1907 Japanese cocktail book *Shiki: Enryo Konseiho* (Four Seasons: How to Mix Drinks) advised that "sake, which is made only for getting drunk, is not suitable for adding flavor to a cocktail."

That may have been true back then. It sure isn't now. Sakes these days are artisanal products that can be sweet, tart, floral, or bone dry. They can be still or sparkling, playing the role of a vermouth or a Prosecco, and more importantly, the best sakes nowadays come without the vicious alcoholic after-bite that would ruin a good drink.

When choosing a brew, the Sake Meter Value gives a rough indication of sweetness. The higher the number, the drier the sake. Anything below zero will usually taste sweet, and above five is likely to be dry.

— L.I.T. —

Sure, it's catnip for tourists, but the L.I.T. (Lost In Translation) cocktail is also a great low-alcohol option in the Cosmopolitan family. Beverage manager Yasukazu Yokota says he wanted to create something with the same sweet-sour balance as the movie, much of which was filmed in this hotel.

GLASSWARE: Cocktail glass

- 1⅓ oz. | 40 ml daiginjo sake
- ⅔ oz. | 20 ml cranberry juice
- 2 bar spoons peach liqueur
- 2 bar spoons sakura liqueur
- 2 bar spoons fresh lime juice

1. Add all of the ingredients to a cocktail shaker with ice, shake vigorously, and strain into a cocktail glass.

– TAIKOH –

Nobuo Abe (see page 92) was running Bar Capri at the Hotel New Otani when the sister-in-law of a famous tea master asked him to create a cocktail for a conference she was organizing there. He combined three of the most auspicious Japanese ingredients—matcha, sake, gold leaf—into something light, sweet, bitter, and delicately tart. The tea master gave the drink its name, which means "aroma of moss."

GLASSWARE: Old Fashioned glass
GARNISH: Edible gold leaf

- 1⅓ oz. | 40 ml sake
- ¾ oz. | 25 ml green tea liqueur
- 1 bar spoon matcha

- 2 bar spoons fresh sudachi or lime juice

1. Add all of the ingredients to a cocktail shaker with ice, shake vigorously, and strain into an Old Fashioned glass filled with ice. Garnish with edible gold leaf.

Abe served this cocktail most recently at Y&M Kisling, though the Ginza bar closed in 2020.

— SHUNGYO —

GINZA TENDER, GINZA

Back in the 1980s, Kazuo Uyeda would create seasonal menus featuring drinks of varying strengths. This one from the fall of 1982 was filed under Strong. The name means "spring dawn," hence the cherry blossom petal garnish.

GLASSWARE: Cocktail glass

GARNISH: Cherry blossom petal

- 1 oz. | 30 ml Smirnoff Vodka
- ½ oz. | 15 ml sake
- 1 bar spoon green tea liqueur

1. Add all of the ingredients to a mixing glass with ice, stir until chilled, and strain into a cocktail glass.

2. Garnish with the cherry blossom petal.

— THE TIME —

OLD IMPERIAL BAR, IMPERIAL HOTEL, YURAKUCHO

In 2017, the Imperial Hotel held a staff contest to design a cocktail for Frank Lloyd Wright's 150th birthday. The great architect had designed an earlier incarnation of the hotel, and remnants of his work decorate the hotel's storied Old Imperial Bar. Chief bartender Nobuaki Sogawa beat more than 30 rivals with a superb recipe combining American and Japanese ingredients for a tart, juicy cousin of a Manhattan.

GLASSWARE: Cocktail glass
GARNISH: Red and green dried ume and gold powder*

- 18 ml Woodford Reserve Bourbon
- 12 ml dry sake
- 30 ml Umenoyado Aragoshi Umeshu

1. Add all of the ingredients to a cocktail shaker with ice, shake vigorously, and strain into a cocktail glass.

2. Garnish with red and green dried ume and gold powder.

Sogawa sprays the ume garnish with gold powder. When he places it in the drink, the gold floats to the surface.

Note: Only metric measurements are used in this recipe to honor its precision.

— TRENCH 75 —

BAR TRENCH, EBISU

Bar Trench's riff on a French 75 was intended as a seasonal special but proved too popular to drop.

GLASSWARE: Coupe
GARNISH: Dehydrated lime wheel

- 1 oz. | 30 ml Nikka Coffey Gin
- ½ oz. | 15 ml fresh lemon juice
- 2 bar spoons Honey Syrup
- 1 oz. | 30 ml Shichiken Sparkling Sake

1. Place the gin, lemon juice, and syrup in a cocktail shaker with ice, shake vigorously, and strain into a coupe. Top with the sparkling sake and garnish with the dehydrated lime wheel.

HONEY SYRUP: Place 1 cup honey and 1 cup water in a saucepan and warm over medium heat, stirring until emulsified. Remove from heat and let cool before using or storing.

BAR TRENCH

When Rogerio Igarashi Vaz came to Tokyo from Sao Paolo, Brazil, at the age of 19, he could speak neither Japanese nor English but found work as a quality controller in a bottle factory north of the capital, checking for defects in containers for everything from cosmetics to umeshu. He was an unlikely candidate for success in the refined world of Tokyo cocktails, and his path didn't become much clearer when he moved to Tokyo and became a waiter in a strip club, but he says that job taught him a lot about service—you have to get your approach just right when your guest has his focus elsewhere.

From there, he moved to an acclaimed tequila bar where he found his love for spirits, and then teamed up with Takuya Ito to open the bars Tram, Trench, and Triad, all within a block of each other in the grown-up nightlife district of Ebisu. Trench is where you'll find the now-trilingual Igarashi Vaz serving original creations, straight-up classics, and revival recipes.

The bar blew fresh air into the Tokyo scene when it opened in 2010. It had menus, and the menus had prices. They even told you how the drinks tasted, and those drinks were playful. It felt like your neighborhood bar, no matter where you lived. On a Monday you could be talking to an avant-garde fashion designer; on the Tuesday a degenerate local barfly. What's remarkable is that it still feels that way after so much global hype and appearances on the World's 50 Best Bars list. Much of that is because of the man behind the stick, whose view of hospitality was influenced by his sister, a hair stylist back in Brazil. She told him: "People don't come to the salon for a haircut. They come to talk. They're getting their hair and nails done, but what they really want is the answer to their relationship problems."

— AJISAI —

MANDARIN BAR, MANDARIN ORIENTAL TOKYO, NIHONBASHI

The hotel with the most Michelin stars dazzles with drinks, too. Fans of the classics decamp to the Oriental Lounge. Those seeking innovation head to the Mandarin Bar, home to more playful drinks like this dry, floral number.

GLASSWARE: Coupe

- 1 oz. | 30 ml Hendrick's Gin
- 1 bar spoon simple syrup
- 1 bar spoon fresh lemon juice
- 1 pinch shiso flowers
- 2 oz. | 60 ml sparkling sake
- Matcha powder, for the rim

1. Rim a coupe with matcha powder and place an ice cube in the glass.

2. Add the gin, syrup, lemon juice, and flowers to a cocktail shaker with ice and shake vigorously.

3. Strain the cocktail into the coupe and top with the sake.

— OOZAKURA —

This drink is so complex you don't notice how light it is. The recipe calls for dekopon, a citrus fruit that's hard to find outside Japan. Any tart-and-sweet orange can work in a pinch.

GLASSWARE: Ceramic cup

GARNISH: Dehydrated cherry blossom petals in simple syrup

- 1½ oz. | 45 ml Mancino Secco Vermouth
- 1 oz. | 30 ml fresh dekopon juice
- ⅔ oz. | 20 ml sweet sake
- 1 bar spoon fresh strawberry juice

1. Combine all the ingredients with ice in a cocktail shaker, shake vigorously, and strain into a ceramic cup.

2. Garnish with the cherry blossom petals.

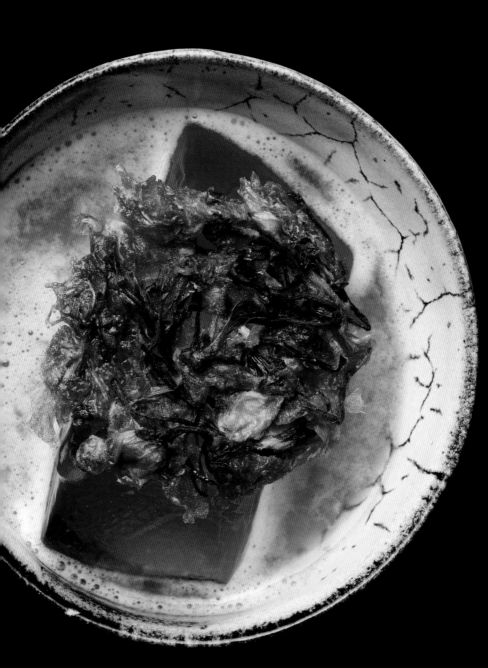

A TASTE OF HISTORY

The first time I visited Bar Evans in Ginza, owner Takamitsu Shibuya made me an excellent Sidecar, but he told me that time was running out on his recipe. The Cointreau he used was from the 1970s and he was down to his last bottle. "In the past you could get bottles like this cheap," he said. "But those days seem to be over." And switching to modern Cointreau was not an option. "It tastes artificial and has no body. The alcohol is all upfront. A good liqueur should have body, with the alcohol behind, pushing it forward."

A few blocks away Taro Ohzama has a similar view. He's a Chartreuse fan who found that the old bottles had more character than the modern ones, and began collecting them. His hobby became an obsession and now his bar, Satin Doll, is crammed with spirits and liqueurs from decades past. As he pours me a glass of deep Kümmel from the 1950s he says it's all gotten a bit out of hand:

"As a responsible bar owner I shouldn't really spend this much on vintage bottles, but that's where all my money goes."

Many of the museum-worthy bottles in Tokyo were imported from Limoges, France, where Karim Karroum runs the rare-alcohol dealership Les Petits Celliers. "No other country has ordered so many old spirits from me," he says. "I think Japan is the only place in the world where it is possible to have a very large choice of bars in which to drink old bottles. For me, the explanation is this: Japanese people are passionate, and when they engage, they totally go for it. And they have understood that the present does not exist without the past."

One of Karroum's customers is Hiroyasu Kayama of Ben Fiddich (see page 254), who says he loves history, the old labels, and finding out what drinks tasted like decades or centuries ago, when methods were so different. His collection includes a Fernet-Branca and Chartreuse from the 1930s and a bottle of an absinthe-like herbal spirit from the 1770s. That last one, he says, is terrible.

Yasutaka Nakamori of Bar Doras in Asakusa and Takahiko Kikuchi of Bar Odin in Ebisu both go straight to the source, touring distilleries in Europe, scouring for treasures. Kikuchi in particular seems to draw no great distinction between a distillery's museum and its gift shop.

"Last October I went to more than 30 places that make Cognac, Armagnac, and Calvados, and tried to buy their bottles from the 1700s," he says. He came back empty-handed that time, but has had success in the past. His collection at the time of writing includes three Cognacs and a Calvados from the 19th century, as well as a mysterious gin from 1919 that he found on a trip to New York.

Bragging rights for the greatest collection, though, belong to Fumihiko Kimura, who runs the bar Kohaku in the former geisha district of Yushima. He estimates that he has 3,000 bottles in his 20-square-meter bar. Most of them have labels that have faded or fallen off. He pours me a Bénédictine that was bottled in the 1950s and I ask how he acquired it. "From my mom," he says. "Every bottle here has only had one owner." Kimura's mother opened the bar in the 1950s and bought so much stock that he's still got some of it.

Kimura agrees that modern spirits and liqueurs lack body and character. "They just don't make alcohol the way they used to," he says. "Young bartenders don't even know what these drinks are supposed to taste like."

Meanwhile, that Cointreau bottle at Bar Evans is empty now, but Shibuya has found a solution. He says the kumquat liqueur by French company Fair is a good surrogate for his old Curaçao: "It doesn't have huge body, but it's so well made that the alcohol doesn't command attention: it stays behind." He still uses a Camus Napoleon Cognac bottled in the 1970s as the base, and the cocktail is still exceptional.

AFTER-DINNER DRINKS

ARCADIA ✦ ETRENNE ✦ CAMILLA ✦

ZACAPA MARTINI ✦ MANHATTAN ✦

TAMAYURA ✦ ORCHARD MANHATTAN

✦ JAPANESE OLD FASHIONED ✦

ADZUKI COCKTAIL ✦ MT. FUJI ✦

TALES OF OCHO ✦ LAST DANCE

It's 9:30 p.m., you've finished dinner, and the only question now is: karaoke or cocktail? Join your office colleagues singing hits by Bump of Chicken and Taylor Swift, or sneak away for a nightcap with the beau monde.

— ARCADIA —

Kiyoshi Shimbashi says he imagined a drink that would turn into a cake if you baked it. This recipe won him a Finlandia vodka cocktail trophy in 1993.

GLASSWARE: Coupe
GARNISH: Crushed Valrhona chocolate and sprig of fresh mint

- ⅔ oz. | 20 ml Finlandia Vodka
- 2 bar spoons Midori Melon Liqueur
- 2 bar spoons Kahlùa
- ⅔ oz. | 20 ml cream
- 1 egg yolk

1. Place all of the ingredients in a cocktail shaker with ice, shake, and strain into a coupe.

2. Garnish with crushed Valrhona chocolate and a sprig of fresh mint.

— ETRENNE —

kihiro Sakoh was only 26 years old when he won the Nippon Bartenders Association's top cocktail prize for this minty dessert drink. A protégé of Takao Mori, he graduated from the Gaslight group to open his eponymous lounge in 2010. Eight years later, he opened a sister branch in Taipei.

GLASSWARE: Cocktail glass
GARNISH: Green cocktail cherry

- ½ oz. | 15 ml vodka
- ⅔ oz. | 20 ml green banana liqueur
- 2 bar spoons mint liqueur
- ½ oz. | 15 ml cream

1. Place all of the ingredients in a cocktail shaker with ice, shake vigorously, and double-strain into a cocktail glass.

2. Garnish with the green cocktail cherry.

— CAMILLA —

It's not just the Laphroaig, a whisky that's "By Appointment to HRH Prince of Wales," that inspired this cocktail's name. Yuichi Hoshi dubbed it "Camilla" because the whisky is an acquired taste and the cocktail isn't pretty enough to be a "Diana." It's a lighter, fruitier, smokier, brilliant rethinking of the Brandy Alexander. Yuichi's son Masaya, who runs the bar one floor above his father's flagship outlet, says it's essential to use a plant-based cream because the dairy stuff makes the drink too heavy. Apologies to British monarchists.

GLASSWARE: Cocktail glass

- ⅔ oz. | 20 ml Laphroaig 10 Year Old Scotch Whisky
- ⅔ oz. | 20 ml Godiva Chocolate Liqueur
- ⅔ oz. | 20 ml nondairy cream
- 1 strip of orange peel

1. Place all of the ingredients in a cocktail shaker with ice, shake, and strain into a cocktail glass.

2. Express the strip of orange peel over the cocktail.

— ZACAPA MARTINI —

BAR HOSHI, GINZA

The Ron Zacapa rum company asked Yuichi Hoshi to make a cocktail with their spirit, and he says he thought of this recipe "immediately." The cherries aren't just for decoration. Eat one and the drink suddenly tastes drier.

GLASSWARE: Old Fashioned glass
GARNISH: 2 griottines

- 55 ml Ron Zacapa 23 Rum
- 1 bar spoon Bulleit Bourbon

1. Place the rum and bourbon in a mixing glass filled with ice, stir until chilled, and strain into an Old Fashioned glass.

2. Garnish with the griottines.

Note: Only metric measurements are used in this recipe to honor its precision.

Yuichi Hoshi was working in Utsunomiya, Ibaraki prefecture in the early 1990s when Takao Mori (see page 34) recommended him for a job in the capital. He moved south and helped open bar Little Smith. Three decades on, Hoshi has built a family of eight bars—four in the same Ginza Building—and won himself an IBA World Championship, but his peers still describe his bartending as "Utsunomiya style" (read: high class, low formality).

— MANHATTAN —

BAR SHERLOCK, GINZA

There used to be a Tokyo bar famed for its Manhattans. It was called Le Verre. Owner Kenichi Sato would stir Old Overholt rye, Cinzano Rosso, and Angostura Bitters with an extra-long spoon that he held at the very top. But Sato moved his bar nearly 500 kilometers north to Akita prefecture in 2008 and there hasn't been an acknowledged Manhattan master in Tokyo since.

There's a hot contender though. Takeshi Yoshimoto of Bar Sherlock makes one that's rich and deep, with balance and body, halfway between silk and velvet. And as with Sato's version, it's partly because of an eye-catching stir.

In Yoshimoto's case, it starts with the smallest mixing glass in Tokyo. He uses a 250-milliliter beaker and just one cube of ice. "You don't need to chill a Manhattan so much," he says. "But you need to mix it, you need an aroma, and you have to get the texture right. It's easier if the drink is cooling slowly."

He stirs briskly, more than 100 times, to marry the ingredients without taking too much water or making it too cold. "With a standard mixing glass you need four ice cubes. But then it chills too quickly and the balance is off," he says.

For most of his career, Yoshimoto mixed Manhattans with traditional tools, but he was never perfectly happy with the outcome.

In 2016, he left the esteemed Bar Four Seasons (no relation to the hotels) and opened Bar Sherlock, furnishing it with blue velvet drapes, brass cobwebs, and just the right amount of detective paraphernalia.

Initially, he bought the miniature beakers as decor, but as he looked at them, he thought they might be the answer to his Manhattan problem. And they were. He also uses them when he makes a Rob Roy, an Affinity, a Hunter, or a Parisian.

The icing on the cake—or the cherry on the bottom—was when he switched the garnish from an artificial cocktail cherry to natural fruit that has rested in a 50/50 mix of syrup and Templeton rye.

GLASSWARE: Cocktail glass
GARNISH: Cherry

- 1½ oz. | 45 ml Templeton rye whiskey
- ½ oz. | 15 ml Mancino Rosso Vermouth
- 3 dashes Angostura Bitters

1. Add the bitters, then the vermouth, then the rye to a small mixing glass containing one ice cube.

2. Stir briskly, more than 100 times.

3. Use the bar spoon to hold the ice cube as you pour the liquid into a cocktail glass. Garnish with the cherry.

— TAMAYURA —

BAR SHAKE, GINZA

Green tea suits chocolate, and chocolate suits whisky. Masako Ikegami connected the dots and won a Suntory Cocktail Award in 2011. She used Hibiki 12 Year Old back then, but since Suntory stopped selling that, she says any other Hibiki works just fine.

GLASSWARE: Cocktail glass

- 1 oz. | 30 ml Suntory Hibiki Blended Whisky
- ½ oz. | 15 ml Hermes Green Tea Liqueur
- ⅓ oz. | 10 ml white chocolate liqueur
- 1 bar spoon cream

1. Place all of the ingredients in a cocktail shaker with ice, shake vigorously, and strain into a cocktail glass.

— ORCHARD MANHATTAN —

BAR ORCHARD, GINZA

This mock Manhattan is devilishly clever and utterly convincing. If you didn't know the recipe, you would never guess.

GLASSWARE: Cocktail glass

GARNISH: 3 cherries

- 1⅔ oz. | 50 ml rye whiskey
- ⅔ oz. | 20 ml Italian red wine
- 2 bar spoons Monin Caramel Syrup
- 1 bar spoon absinthe
- 2 dashes Dr. Adam Elmegirab's Boker's Bitters
- 1 dash Angostura Bitters
- 1 strip of orange zest

1. Add all of the ingredients to a mixing glass with ice, stir until chilled, and strain into a cocktail glass.

2. Garnish with the cherries.

— JAPANESE OLD FASHIONED —

BAR ISHINOHANA, SHIBUYA

A shiitake mushroom infusion turns the Old Fashioned into an umami bomb. The bitters, by a company called The Japanese Bitters, contain kelp, bonito, and shiitake.

GLASSWARE: Old Fashioned glass
GARNISH: Slice of shiitake mushroom

- 1½ oz. | 45 ml Shiitake-Infused Hakushu Whisky
- 1 dash The Japanese Bitters Umami Bitters
- 1 bar spoon maple syrup

1. Place all of the ingredients in a mixing glass filled with ice, stir until chilled, and strain into an Old Fashioned glass filled with ice.

2. Garnish with the slice of mushroom.

SHIITAKE-INFUSED HAKUSHU WHISKY: Ishigaki keeps the proportions of his infusion a secret, but he will reveal that steeping for 36 hours yields the best results.

— ADZUKI COCKTAIL —

BAR LEGACY, SHIBUYA

Wwhat says "Japanese dessert" more than adzuki beans? Atsushi Yoshikawa pairs Hokkaido beans with a Hokkaido whisky, and a milk made from beans.

GLASSWARE: Cocktail glass
GARNISH: Rose petal and edible gold leaf

- 1⅓ oz. | 40 g adzuki beans
- 1 oz. | 30 ml Nikka Yoichi Single Malt Whisky
- 3 oz. | 90 ml soy milk
- 1 bar spoon brown sugar simple syrup

1. Add all of the ingredients to a container and combine with a hand blender.

2. Pour the mixture into a Boston shaker, add ice, and shake briefly.

3. Double-strain into a cocktail glass and garnish with a rose petal and edible gold leaf.

— MT. FUJI —

OLD IMPERIAL BAR, IMPERIAL HOTEL TOKYO,
YURAKUCHO

The precise recipe for the Imperial Hotel's most famous cocktail is a secret. The ingredients are listed on the bar's menu, but the ratios have never been revealed.

The origin of the Mt. Fuji is something of a mystery too. Imperial Hotel representatives say it was created in 1924 to welcome visitors who were on a round-the-world voyage. At that time, only the world's wealthiest people—titans of industry and movie stars—could afford to take such a trip, so the hotel wanted to put on a show. But that's as far as the official story goes. Imperial Hotel records don't note who invented the drink, or even who was bartending in that era.

In 2013, though, Japanese drink writer Kazuo Ishikura wrote a lengthy essay about his mission to identify the unsung hero. Using interviews, anecdotes, old menus, vintage cocktail books, and some educated guesswork, he concluded that the inventor was a bartender named Takaaki Osaka, who had trained at the luxurious Tor Hotel in Kobe before being scouted by the manager of the Imperial Hotel.

The bartenders at the Old Imperial Bar pour the cocktail by eye, not jigger, so there is no way to ascertain the recipe by spying, but the taste suggests a healthy pour of gin and a restrained amount of the other ingredients.

GLASSWARE: Coupe

GARNISH: Maraschino cherry

- A good amount of Hayman's Old Tom gin
- A little fresh lemon juice
- A little egg white
- Very little maraschino liqueur
- Very little pineapple juice
- Very little cream
- Dash of simple syrup

1. Place all of the ingredients in a cocktail shaker with ice, shake vigorously, and strain into a coupe.

2. Garnish with the maraschino cherry.

— TALES OF OCHO —

SKY GALLERY LOUNGE LEVITA,
THE PRINCE GALLERY TOKYO KIOICHO, AKASAKA

Using a snifter instead of a cocktail glass was a clever touch—you could nose this beauty for an hour. It won Akira Abe the Japan heat of the Bacardi Legacy contest in 2018 and put his hotel bar on the Tokyo cocktail map.

GLASSWARE: Brandy snifter

GARNISH: Finely ground coffee

- 1⅔ oz. | 50 ml Bacardi Reserva Ocho
- 1 oz. | 30 ml brewed espresso
- ½ oz. | 15 ml demerara sugar syrup
- 8 fresh mint leaves
- 1⅓ oz. | 40 ml sparkling wine

1. Place all of the ingredients, except for the sparkling wine, in a cocktail shaker filled with ice, shake vigorously, and strain into a brandy snifter.

2. Top with the sparkling wine and garnish with the coffee powder.

— LAST DANCE —

GASLIGHT BARS

It would be hard to overstate the importance of Gaslight Kasumigas-eki. Some of the city's legends, including Takao Mori (see page 34) and Atsushi Asakura (see page 46) have run the place. It has grown to a quartet of bars under the eye of Noriyuki Iguchi, a man most famous for his Martini. He probably won't mention that he won the 2007 Nippon Bartenders Association cocktail contest by figuring out that Calvados and chestnuts are a dream combination.

GLASSWARE: Cocktail glass

- ⅔ oz. | 20 ml Calvados
- ½ oz. | 15 ml mint liqueur
- ½ oz. | 15 ml cream
- 2 bar spoons Monin Chestnut Syrup

1. Place all of the ingredients in a cocktail shaker with ice, shake vigorously, and double strain into a cocktail glass.

— SAZERAC —

Hidetsugu Ueno's Japanese Sazerac uses all local ingredients, including an absinthe from Kyoto, the high-proof whisky Nikka From The Barrel, and a Nikka brandy. His homemade yuzu bitters bring the citrus notes, so there's no need for the traditional lemon peel garnish.

GLASSWARE: Old Fashioned glass

- Absinthe, to rinse
- 1⅓ oz. | 40 ml Nikka From The Barrel Whisky
- ⅔ oz. | 20 ml Nikka XO Deluxe Brandy
- 2 bar spoons simple syrup
- 1 bar spoon Yuzu Peel Bitters

1. Rinse an Old Fashioned glass with absinthe.

2. Place two large ice cubes in the glass and stir. Discard the top cube.

3. Add the remaining ingredients and stir until chilled. Remove and discard the remaining ice cube.

YUZU PEEL BITTERS: Peel a yuzu and dry the peel. Ueno places the peel in front of a fan for a day or two to get it to the proper level of dryness. Cram as much of the peel as possible into a jar and fill it with high-proof vodka. Let the mixture sit for 6 months. Strain before using or storing.

— BRANDY ALEXANDER —

BAR DORAS, ASAKUSA

At Bar Doras, a block from the tourist maelstrom of Asakusa, Yasutaka Nakamori serves his Cognacs with chasers of chilled Earl Grey tea, not water, because water is too *wet*. "A wet mouth makes a Cognac taste harsh," he says.

That sounded unlikely, so I tested the idea—at home, in private, to be polite. He is astonishingly correct. Water ruins a brandy; Earl Grey does not.

All of which is to say that Nakamori knows an awful lot about Cognac. He takes annual study trips to the region, has written a book about those adventures, has amassed an impressive collection of bottles, and is known citywide as the man to see about distilled wine.

Nakamori says it is harder to pour a glass of Cognac, getting the temperature, glass, and chaser just right, than it is to make a cocktail.

He says the Cognacs and Scotches in his bar are the entrees; cocktails are the appetizers and desserts. A sensible menu might begin with a Sidecar or a Champs-Elysees, followed by a Cognac main course, and his exceptional Brandy Alexander for pudding.

Nakamori's cocktail philosophy, common in Tokyo, is that beginners reach for expensive craft spirits, pros can get the same results with standard bottles. But he says you shouldn't go too standard with the Cognac. The most famous brands have sugar and caramel added to make them more approachable and more compatible with ice and water. He wants something more elegant, so he uses a Frapin VSOP from the Grand Champagne region.

But using an unsweetened Cognac is harder, precisely because of that wetness problem. The solution is in the shake. Use a Cobbler shaker and make sure the top never points downward because that will produce a watery drink. Use smaller than usual ice with rounded corners and leave some space in the shaker. Hold it squarely in front of you, and when you shake, bring the ice back before it hits the bottom of the shaker. Twist it with your wrist as you go, and Nakamori says you can shake longer than usual and create fine bubbles without adding much water. If you pour correctly—drawing circles with the shaker rather than jabbing or rattling it—you don't need to double-strain and you will achieve a superb texture.

The other secret to the Doras Alexander is a little Port wine, which sweetens the drink and provides a deliciously long, figgy finish. And his answer to the nutmeg-or-not question? Do it. But only if you grate it freshly from the seed.

GLASSWARE: Coupe

GARNISH: Freshly grated nutmeg

- 22 ml Frapin VSOP
- 15 ml Eyguebelle Liqueur de Cacao Blanc
- 8 ml Tawny Port
- 20 ml cream
- 3 drops Bitter Truth Chocolate Bitters

1. Place all of the ingredients, except the bitters, in a cocktail shaker and blend with a bar spoon.

2. Add ice, shake vigorously, and strain into a coupe.

3. Grate the nutmeg over the drink and add the bitters.

Note: Only metric measurements are used in this recipe to honor its precision.

viper rebirth

BAR LANDSCAPE

Birdsong, soulful music,
the song turns landscape,
an aria of tastes.
Today too birds will sing.
I will journey anew.

CÁDIZ BAR

4Cs Bar Rosso

SUZU BAR

open

TRENCH

APPENDIX

WHERE TO BUY TOOLS
OF THE TRADE IN TOKYO

BAR TIMES STORE
5-1-8 Ginza, Chuo-ku
bar-times-store.tokyo

Bar Times began in 2011 as a free magazine focused on bartending. In 2012, it morphed into a web-only magazine at bar-times.com, where it continues to publish features on the Japanese bar scene. The bar tools brick-and-mortar arrived in 2014, offering 75 styles of cocktail shaker, pistol-grip ice knives, and Japanese *usuhari* ultra-thin glassware among many other items. The English-speaking staff, and proximity to many of Tokyo's greatest bars, have made this a favorite of visiting bartenders.

SOKICHI
2-1-14 Kaminarimon, Taito-ku
sokichi.co.jp

Ask a Tokyo bartender where they shop, and the answer is often "Sokichi, of course." Owner Kichigoro Sekibe began 30 years ago as an itinerant salesman going from bar to bar selling glassware. Since he opened his store around the turn of the millennium, the bartenders go to him. He offers a mix of Japanese and European glassware and bar tools, new and antique. He can also engrave or print on your glasses. If you wish to try your hand at carving glassware with traditional Edo-kiriko patterns, head upstairs where there are 36 workstations and expert teachers.

SUGAHARA

3-10-18 Kita-Aoyama, Minato-ku

sugahara.co.jp

Several of the glasses photographed for this book were handmade by the artisans of Sugahara, a company that has been in business since 1932. The showroom in Aoyama has the best of their collection. At their factory in Chiba prefecture, next to Tokyo, you can take classes in glass blowing and stretching.

TSUBAYA

3-7-2 Nishi-Asakusa, Taito-ku

tsubaya.co.jp

Kappabashi Street in Asakusa has knife shops galore. The pick of the bunch is Tsubaya, established in the 1950s as a general homeware store, but transformed by the founder's son into a knife specialist with more than 1,000 blades. The English-speaking staff can tell you which are best for cutting lemons and which to use for carving ice.

PHOTO CREDITS

Pages 3, 12-13 used under official license from Shutterstock.com; pages 4-5, 16, 30-31, 52, 55, 57, 66-67, 72, 75, 76, 81, 82, 85, 86, 94-95, 102, 104, 107, 110, 134, 138, 141, 158, 184-185, 193, 275, 280-281, 291, 292, 296-297, 300 , 323, 345 by Marika Rinno; pages 6, 8-10 courtesy of Library of Congress; pages 15, 18, 30-31, 35-36, 38, 41-42, 46-47, 49, 58, 61, 90, 98, 108, 116, 119, 130, 133, 144, 147-148, 155-156, 160, 163, 165-166, 168-169, 172, 179, 180-181, 186, 189, 198, 202, 204, 206, 208-209, 216, 219, 227, 234, 236, 239-240, 243, 247-248, 254-255, 257-258, 261, 264-265, 273, 278, 302, 304, 309-310, 320, 324, 327-328, 330, 332, 336, 346, 347, 357-357 by Juan Qi An; 63 courtesy Suntory; pages 64-65, 100, 137, 152, 213, 215, 228, 231, 244, 251, 307, 339, 342 by Nicholas Coldicott; pages 112-113 by Hiromichi Itabashi; page 114 by Yusuke Takamiya; pages 121, 122 courtesy The Kyoto Distillery; page 123 courtesy Shohei Tatsumi; pages 126-127, 313 courtesy Mandarin Oriental Tokyo; pages 174-175 courtesy The Palace Hotel Tokyo; pages 194, 197, 335 by You Jin Lee; page 222 courtesy Pullman Tokyo Tamachi; pages 232, 316-317 courtesy Hotel New Otani Tokyo; pages 252, 288 courtesy The SG Club; pages 269, 270, 287 courtesy Shuzo Nagumo; page 341 courtesy Akira Abe; pages 352-353 courtesy Bar Times Store.

ABOUT THE AUTHOR

Nicholas Coldicott moved from London to Tokyo in 1998 and has been writing about the Japanese drinks scene for almost that long. He is a former drink columnist for *The Japan Times* and CNN, a former editor of *Eat Magazine* and *Whisky Magazine Japan*, and writer of guide books for Wallpaper and Time Out. He is also co-founder of craft sake exporters KuroKura.

He would like to thank Chikako Tanaka, Marika Rinno, Juan Qi An, Hu Jia Jiong, Kate Crockett, Mari Minamide, Tomoko Yoshizawa, Miguel Quintana, Shu Kuge, Hiroyuki Miura, Mika Kim, Saori Shiobara, Yuki Inoue, and Hiromitsu Ito.

INDEX

—ABOUT CIDER MILL PRESS BOOK PUBLISHERS—

Good ideas ripen with time. From seed to harvest, Cider Mill Press brings fine reading, information, and entertainment together between the covers of its creatively crafted books. Our Cider Mill bears fruit twice a year, publishing a new crop of titles each spring and fall.

BOOK
PUBLISHERS
KENNEBUNKPORT, MAINE

"Where Good Books Are Ready for Press"

Visit us on the web at
cidermillpress.com

or write to us at
PO Box 454
12 Spring St.
Kennebunkport, Maine 04046